Love, Good Karma

Love, Good Karma

Nicki Davis

K8ND Publishing

Inspired by a true story. Some names, characters, places, and incidents are the products of the author's imagination. Anything in this book that could get the author in trouble is simply not true.

Printed in the USA.
ISBN: 978-1-7341042-0-2

Published by K8ND Publishing 2020

To my nephew, because every step along the journey is better with paw prints.

And to every furry addition—welcome, Ace!

karma |ˈkärmə| noun

(In Hinduism and Buddhism) The term karma is derived from Sanskrit, the primary language of Hinduism, and is defined as **action, effect**, and **fate**. It is the sum of a person's actions in this and previous states of existence, viewed as deciding their fate in future existences.

Contents

Hello, my human friend,

Have you ever rubbed a dog's belly?
  We roll over onto our backs and you rhythmically move your hand back and forth, running your fingers through our warm fur. For a moment, it's quiet. Then you hear a hum, m-m-m-m, a sound like a boat idling. M-m-m-m. Essentially, you are sharing a connection. Dogs like me experience pure bliss, and in return, your shoulders relax, you forget about your problems, and you smile at love.
  And love is at the center of this story, so let's take this journey together. I can

sit by your side as you turn the page or I can lead the way.

Has your heart ever skipped a beat? Have you felt trapped, like you can't breathe? Are you lousy at life and relationships? Looking for love, or moving on?

Everyone has a story . . .

Love,
Good Karma

Part 1—Flight Risk

Karma means action.
So things change through action,
not by prayer . . . not by wish.
—His Holiness,
the fourteenth Dalai Lama

The First Law of Karma:
The Great Law

What We Put Out into the Universe Will
Come Back to Us

Cause and effect

Finding Karma

It was October 1, 2008, on a Southwest Florida evening beneath a blazing sky—my favorite time of the day. Orange-gold and violet-red splashed across the horizon, and there was a hint of a blue-gray night beyond the scattered clouds. Maybe there's a rare person out there in the world who could tire of tranquil ocean waves and colorful skies, but I've never met one. This piece of paradise called to me almost twenty-six years ago—a place different in almost every way from my childhood home in England.

Doug and I had finished work early again. Our office was starting to feel the effects of the real estate financial meltdown. With only the odd booking for a showing here and there, we had time to play tennis, ride our bikes, or go boating and fishing right from our backyard. He had surprised me a year earlier with a new set of wheels that had multiple gears. Now I no longer had an excuse to not keep up.

But the salt air had worked its way into the chain. We stopped short of the driveway and turned back so Doug could spray a little oil in just the right spot. As he reached down to tend to the squeak, I didn't even get off my bike. I knew he'd have us sorted, and we'd be back on the path in a flash. He stood up, a solid six feet tall, tanned, fit, and handsome, and a smile spread across my face as I admired my love of fifteen years.

"My hero," I flirted.

Doug reached over and gave me a kiss. "Let's try this again."

At first our attention was centered on the chain, waiting to see if it would protest once again, but then our focus was drawn to a flutter in the tree line at the edge of the golf course near our house. They were back! The bald eagles were home.

The smaller of the two majestic birds rested on a high branch, surveying the nest. It must have been the male. I had read once that females could be a solid five to seven inches longer than their mates. The larger bird, presumably the female in this partnership, was in their nest. Her blackish-brown feathers shimmered in the remnants of sunlight. These incredible creatures were so impressive to me with their white heads, necks, and tails. They were so close that I could even make out the male's yellow feet and beak.

We remained motionless for several minutes, and exchanged no words. But I knew we were feeling the exact same thing: the privilege of watching the simplicity and perfection of nature, appreciating the innate cycle of life and the understanding of divine partnership. It was Doug's turn to look at me with a smile. It started first in his eyes, then worked its way to the sides of his mouth. The eagle spread her wings, five feet across. She took flight—and made me jump! as she flew by me. Catching a sudden current, she soared from the nest, over our heads, and out toward the ocean waves. What a moment! How wonderful to leap from a perch with such faith and grace. To soar without fear and trust that your wings will carry you wherever you choose to go.

Mesmerized, I almost didn't hear Doug's question at first. He asked it again.

"Did you see the classified page in the newspaper today?" His voice pulled me back to our bikes and the fading light.

He always read our local newspaper cover to cover, except for the classified section. "For some reason the classifieds caught my eye today," he continued.

Instantly, I knew what he was going to say next. Just the week before Doug had brought up an idea—that if and when I felt ready again, our next dog might be a Maltese. We'd had an encounter with some vacationers down the street from us who had brought with them a black-and-white shih tzu named Sophie. She was adorable. She reminded me a great deal of my first dog, Cheena; her fur was the exact same coloring.

"What did the ad say?" I asked.

"Maltese/shih tzu puppies for sale," Doug replied.

That was an interesting combination, but I'd put the thought of a new dog out of my mind for most of the week. The idea overwhelmed me. Cheena had passed on nearly four years prior, and I still missed her terribly. How could any other dog compare?

I looked up to the nest, contemplating what to say next, and remembered a conversation I'd had while driving with my four-year-old niece after Cheena died.

"Where did Cheena go?" she asked.

"She went home to heaven. Heaven shared her with us for thirteen years," I replied.

"Does heaven have other dogs too?" she asked.

"Yes, darling."

I could see her in my rearview mirror as she stared out the window.

She turned to me and asked, "Where is heaven?"

"With God," I said. "And because dogs are so special, they have the same letters to spell their name. G–O–D spelled backward is D–O–G." Her gaze went back to the window and up toward the sky. Satisfied, her mind moved on, but mine didn't.

There's so much to learn from a D–O–G. They naturally live in the moment, which seems such a hard place for us humans to be. We're always living in the past or running to the future. Sometimes the thought of Cheena made me smile; other times, it made me tear up as I remembered that I had ended her life. Her impact on me was immense. For thirteen years, she had kept me grounded and given me direction.

No one is exempt from the pain of losing a beloved friend. It's a time when rags and riches are all dealt the same hand: love bursting at the seams from a broken heart. Now, nearly four years later, could I let another dog into my life, knowing it might mean I would one day have to make that heart-breaking decision again?

"I'd like to see that ad," I said. We turned our bikes around and headed straight for home.

. . .

I dialed the number and a brash female voice answered. For a moment I questioned my new resolve. I glanced at the ad again: "Eight-week-old Maltese/shih tzu puppies for sale." I did my best to swallow the hesitation in my voice. "I'm calling about the puppies. Are they still available?"

The woman on the other end didn't hesitate; the reply was terse. "Two boys and two girls."

Was I really about to have this conversation? Excitement mixed with fear was building inside me by the second. "I'd be interested in the little girls. What color are they?" It was as if someone else was asking the questions.

"One's a mix of black and white, the other's all white, with little gold-y flecks on her face," the woman said.

"Gold flecks?"

"Sure, you know, like beige-y ginger-y specks of fur."

"The white one with gold, can I come by and see her tomorrow?" I asked, realizing the black-and-white one would look too much like Cheena.

My mind still felt guarded and unsure, but my body was overcome with adrenaline and an incredible sense of urgency. Now that I'd taken this step, the thought of someone else scooping up this puppy absolutely tormented me.

"Not tomorrow," she replied. "How about Saturday?"

"No, tomorrow." It was my turn to be terse.

"Oh, all right, fine then. When I get home from work."

"I'll be there." I knew it would be a long wait through the day, but I would take what I could get. At least we weren't waiting until Saturday!

Just then Doug walked into the room. I did my best to act casual, trying to convince both Doug and myself—okay, mostly myself—that this was just a starting place. Whenever we made an important decision, it always took time and research, so why would this be any different?

"Let's just go and see," I said.

"Let's just go and see," he replied, flashing that wonderful reassuring smile at me again.

That night I lay awake for hours; the waiting seemed like an eternity. It was almost as if I could hear a voice in my mind. It's time to embrace your karma . . .

That was it! I woke Doug.

"Doug! Doug! Her name just came to me. Karma! It's Good Karma!"

"We'll know it when we see her," he whispered, then fell back to sleep.

I sat up and looked around the bedroom. My thoughts were moving in every direction. *Get it together, Nicki. Take this one step at a time. You don't have any dog supplies. You haven't checked with the vet. You've already named her and you haven't even seen her yet!* But the memory of puppy breath and soft puppy fur flooded my senses. Somehow, on some level beyond my crazy inner dialogue, I just knew that everything would be as it was meant to be. I closed my eyes and fell asleep.

. . .

A few hours later I woke to birds singing and sun streaming into our room. Regardless of the lack of sleep, I still felt fresh and eager to prepare for this new endeavor. I went about my day as usual, adding a call to the vet to see how quickly we could get an appointment. Before I knew it, it was time for us to visit the puppies. As Doug drove us to the neighboring town, half an hour away, I crumbled again.

My palms were wet, and I felt dizzy. My mind took over, sending paralyzing fear through my body, replacing the calm and joyful anticipation I had felt during the day. It was all becoming real now. This time yesterday none of this had even been a consideration. It was as if every one of my cells had stepped up and said: "Do you remember how painful it was to lose Cheena? Can you really risk that kind of hurt again? You should protect yourself! Don't do it." I felt sick to my stomach. I had to change my focus. *Just breathe*, I told myself. I asked the universe, in its great wisdom, for a favor—if this puppy is not meant to be, please have someone else choose her before we get there. It was the best I could do. I needed to trust that something bigger was at play in this decision.

We arrived early and were prepared to wait in the car until the appointed time, but a woman was standing in the driveway. Checking the wrinkled piece of paper in my sweaty palm, I confirmed the address. We got out of the car and introduced ourselves.

"Are you the owner of puppies for sale?" I asked.

"No," she replied. "I'm here to see them." My stomach jumped back onto the roller coaster. Breathe. Breathe.

We both had an appointment at the same time. Oh, crap, I thought. The woman went on to introduce herself to us, explaining that she was going to surprise her son and husband with a dog, but that she was only planning to look today.

I focused on my breathing again.

At 4:45 p.m., the puppy owner greeted us. Her home was small and tidy. Judging by the framed portraits adorning the crochet-covered coffee table and bookshelf, it was obvious that she cared for and loved her three dogs and four pups. We were directed past the kitchen to a screened-in back porch. The woman who was "just looking" rushed straight onto the small lanai where four cute puppies were secured in a padded pen. The puppy's mum, a shih tzu and Maltese mix, was taking a break from the frisky litter, while the father, a Maltese, followed us around, desperate for attention. A black standard poodle oversaw the scene, seeming to stand guard over each of the tiny new additions.

The puppies looked to be all of two pounds. My heart almost burst when I saw their delicate noses and watched their wiggly fur bottoms as they vied for space beside one another. The other lady stepped into this picture-perfect scene and abruptly picked up her prize without a second thought. I scanned the puppy in her arms. It was one of the girls, the black-and-white one! To my amazement, the woman left with the puppy within minutes. The universe had provided me with the information I had requested.

There were two boys and the one girl left. She was a small white bundle of fur, curled up in a corner, paying little attention to her brothers, who were busy attacking my shoelaces. She looked calm and cool, as if she had been expecting us, not trembling like her sister had been. Suddenly, she stretched her legs, yawned, and looked directly at me.

I picked her up. She was tiny enough to fit in my hands. As I smoothed her soft white fur, I whispered, "Karmaaaa."

She tilted her head to one side as though she actually understood me and already knew her name. Doug and I looked at each other. Our hearts melted, and our fate was sealed. It hadn't been my intention to take her home on the first visit, any more than it was the other woman's plan. But there was no way I was leaving without her.

It's interesting to me how easy it is to get in

my own way sometimes. From that moment on, she would remind me every day of the first law of karma: what we put out into the universe will come back to us.

As our car approached the Marco Bridge, I told Karma that her first trip over it would be an amazing adventure. Then I smiled as I remembered my own.

I am Karma, Nicki's dog. Welcome to our story.

In this book Nicki shares stories that shine a light on the lessons of karma, that integral part of the human passage. I'm not talking about myself, Karma the dog (Good Karma is my full name, and Nicki calls me that all the time). I'm talking about a universal-operating-system-that-teaches-us-responsibility-for-our-lives kind of karma. You'll hear from me too; in every chapter I'll tell you a story of my own.

When I first came into Nicki's life, she didn't yet know whether events unfolded for her the way they did because of karma—because of the energy set in motion by imprints made in the past—or if fate was simply leading her to the destiny it had in mind for her. If it was karma that influenced her life, she wondered, could she rewrite the echoes of past decisions?

My instinct tells me that good karma is about

love showing us what we need to know so we can move forward in the direction of our dreams. It's about pushing past fear and shining our light into the world. Dogs on this earth just have the inside scoop on such matters. One of the great things about being a canine is that I'm wired to choose happiness and love. I have a leg up (pun intended) on our two-legged companions when it comes to love.

For humans, finding that sweet spot isn't always so easy. For some reason they have difficulty staying in the happy space that comes so naturally to me, especially once they grow up. They seem to have an area in their brain that hangs on to fear. Fear of pain, loss, or rejection. The sad thing I have learned by being around humans is that fear only serves to hold them back from sowing the energetic seeds of love, joy, and acceptance.

As I head to my chair to fetch my favorite toy kitten, pink with gray-tipped ears and tail, my human is looking at her note pad and trying to concentrate, one elbow on the table, her head tilted and resting in her hand. She is writing of the choices she made so very long ago, and I think she is working hard to clearly see, in her mind's eye, those moments of choosing. I offer her my magic kitten. It always makes me feel happy and peaceful, and I can tell by her smile that it works on her too.

Nicki is studying the first and most significant of the twelve karmic laws: the law of cause and effect. It helps her understand the lessons of her life journey.

Almost every religion mentions the laws of karma in one sense or another—the Bible, the Qur'an, and the Hindu and Buddhist writings. But to me, karma is just like Newton's law that says every action must have a reaction. Life truly does seem to be nothing more than a series of actions and reactions. My friend Jake would say the only control any of us really has is in the way we react to our surroundings. All our thoughts, actions, and feelings—whether conscious or unconscious—are reactions to events within our environment. Every time we bark, bite, or have a thought, we're putting energy out into the world, which then reflects back to us. Some people say that the law of cause and effect is a reward-and-punishment system, but I don't see it that way. It's more of an energy exchange that, when consciously harnessed, can create opportunities to learn and grow. So, if we want to create love and happiness, we have to learn to sow the seeds of those same things.

You might ask, How does one make the right choices to promote good karma? There's an impressive human teacher (and confessed admirer of canines) who once said that even when you think you have your life all mapped out, things happen that shape your destiny in ways you might never have imagined. That human's name is something like . . . Deebark Chopruff, I think. Clearly, he's a clever human, and I couldn't agree with him more.

Thankfully, Nicki was able to overcome the loss of one of the greatest loves she had ever known. In doing so, she trusted her heart again and made a choice that would allow fate—and good karma—to find her.

The Second Law of Karma: Creation

Life Doesn't Happen by Itself—
We Need to Make It Happen

Action creates change

Have you ever tried to catch the invisible force that comes out of those plugged-in hand gadgets that help your hair dry faster? It's real; I can feel it. It's like dozens of feathers fluffing my soft white fur and tickling my skin. I can fill my mouth with its loud warm air, gulp at it, and even sneeze it from the back of my throat out to the end of my nose. Try as I might, though, I can never swallow anything that justifies the effort it takes to catch that invisible power.

How do I know about wet hair, you ask? When my humans are finished working, I get to run and roll my way across the beautiful grass carpet where people whack those little white balls. Humans call it a golf course, but I call it heaven! But as fun as balls and sticks are, what I look forward to the most during this early evening ritual is chasing wood storks and blue herons across the sand traps. Like a lion in tall grass, I feel my animal reflexes kick in, and I dive-bomb into the soft brush for prey. One of these days, I know I will catch one of them! Then I return home with my humans, who praise my noble hunting efforts even as they put me in the sink to wash—and later blow-dry—my muddied coat.

Today I'm watching Nicki from my favorite spot on our enclosed front porch. It's a room fixed up just for me, with glass doors to the outside world. Nicki is once again writing her story, wondering how the karmic laws have played their part in our journey. I can tell that this is not an easy thing to do, because the theory of karma suggests that we take personal responsibility for the bumps in our road. This can be a tricky concept to chew on.

I don't think a creature on this planet will live a full life without feeling some sort of sadness. So, does karma mean we are at fault when we come across hard times? Or can we say that challenge is our opportunity to make something different happen—an opportunity to participate in the act of creation itself?

Nicki may not have been consciously aware of these ideas when she was growing up. She may not have known the importance of each step along her path—both the good experiences and the bad. I suspect, however, that as she puts her story together, she will begin to see the importance of each experience. Each was a piece of the puzzle of her life, slipping into place.

In the Beginning

Other than a secondary school enrollment at a Catholic convent for girls, my mum went to the same schools as my dad when they were growing up. They also attended the same youth club, where my dad outscored everyone at table tennis on Saturday afternoons—everyone except my mum, that is. She was his match, but given that he was head-over-heels in love with her, perhaps he let her win. At twenty-one, they were married. My mum moved one whole mile to her new home at 31 Warren Avenue, a few miles southeast of London, England, in a town called Bromley. This was the house I was brought home to after my birth in the early 60s, and I would live there for my first twenty-one years.

There were five of us in our two-story, three-bedroom home. I remember well the winter mornings when my brother and sister raced for the one bathroom. I stayed put in bed, waiting on Mum to turn up the radiators and get breakfast started. She was always busy with endless cooking, cleaning, and washing, and never once expected us to help.

Her most treasured wedding present was an ironing board with a custom seat. It was so well built that decades later it still invited onlookers to marvel, "They don't make boards like this anymore." There's not a day I remember that she wasn't sitting at that immaculate contraption, sorting through our clothes after pulling them off the line. She never complained, but then most women didn't where I came from. Stoic Englishwomen, they were too proud to show emotions or wear their problems on their sleeves. For some reason it made me feel sad to see her sit at that board day after day. As far back as I can remember, I swore to myself that one day I would have my very own bathroom and a life that didn't require me to wake up early on cold mornings.

Maybe I was bored, wanting a more dynamic life than the one my mother had. Despite the unwavering support and strength that my family always provided, I longed for something different, and I got my start at breaking the mold early.

Half a mile away, in the village of Shortlands at the bottom of Swan Hill, stood the Valley School. This is where I started my primary education; it was the same school my brother had attended two years before me, and my sister, six years after. It was during my final year at Valley School that my favorite teacher, Mrs. Flowers, was fired. Unbelievably, she was let go for being overweight. She didn't have a car; she couldn't fit into one. Instead, she walked Swan Hill each day, back and forth to school. In the classroom she made us laugh, reading us books like *Little Women* and *Charlie and the Chocolate Factory*, pulling us into rich tapestries of imagination and words. We didn't care that her body didn't fit the mold that the other teachers and parents expected, or that her clothes were unlike anyone else's because she had to have them custom-tailored. She cared deeply about her students, and loved what she did. She brought so much life to the classroom each day that she made it exciting to come to school.

The day she was fired was the day I lost interest in sitting in a classroom. Even at such a young age, I could see how small-minded our school system could be, and by extension how small my hometown would soon feel to me. I wondered if Mrs. Flowers would ever find another job so close to her home again, and if not, what she would do. I would never forget what the system had stolen from my teacher, and what it had taken from me.

The system wouldn't turn out any better at my next school, only now we students were older and more defiant. The school supplied textbooks with answers in the back. If all you had to do was turn the book upside down to find the right answer, where was the incentive to learn? One day we watched as one teacher drove her car straight into the wall that surrounded the school. She should have retired years earlier, yet the system allowed her to teach a math class. She couldn't even see who was in class, so it was easy to skip it, and many of us did.

Attending Aylesbury School for Girls, a secondary school, meant a change in my world. As always, I was one of the youngest in my class. I found little connection with my new teachers. At first I attended all of my classes, but eventually boredom won out. I found myself jumping over the school wall to join friends in Bromley's Market Square. At the local coffee shop, when we should have been in class, we gorged ourselves on hot-from-the-oven breads and soup, followed by a cream slice (a pastry layered with fresh cream and jam). Like most teens, we instinctually focused on getting through this hormonally awkward time of life as quickly as possible.

Somewhere deep in my spirit, I knew that I was different, that I couldn't follow the stepping stones of Bromley life with ease the way everyone else did. I wanted to find my heart's purpose in this life. And for that journey, I needed a bigger world to explore.

Exactly how that would unfold, I did not know as a young girl—those would be choices to make as I grew to adulthood. Meanwhile, I enjoyed the rhythms and rituals of my hometown life. Spring brought daffodils and tulips, and the evenings grew longer. We rode our bikes to the park to play rounders. Summer brought even more light, and birthday celebrations in the garden as rose bushes bloomed everywhere. Then the excitement of packing our suitcases for warm holidays in Spain. There were bonfires under dark skies on November 5th as we lit up Guy Fawkes night, eating sausages and warming our hands.

Yet none of these memories holds a candle to my most treasured memory of all—Christmas! On Christmas nights, my family—cousins, aunts, and uncles—would get together at my grand-parents' house. I'd sit next to the giant artificial snowman in the living room, tilting my head to look up at his top hat, for I knew that the head of this massive snowman would actually come off, revealing a bounty of presents inside. Above us, over the door, hung a giant traditional Christmas cracker. We stayed up until midnight, every last one of us, waiting for the moment the bell would ring and Father Christmas—an English Santa—would appear at the door.

As soon as the doorbell rang, the race was on. It didn't really matter who won because somehow the man in the red suit and white beard knew exactly which big, special gift everyone was hoping for. Like my first talking doll. She was large, almost the size of me, and you could pull a string at her back to make her talk. Another present I got from my granddad, aka Father Christmas, was a record player, and my love of music was born.

At that time, I had no idea that this wasn't what every child experienced at Christmas, an evening spent sitting around, opening presents beside their grandparents' tree. The tree shined so brightly that even when I went to bed and closed my eyes, I could still see its silver-and-gold shimmer.

Now, as I look back, I can see the depth of my connections to that time of year. Such holiday traditions forged the bonds of family, faith, and belief. They were an avenue for me to find self-esteem as a child. I got up on that day and knew that I was special. Back then, I don't think I would have been able to comprehend that Father Christmas did not consider all children equally, that he did not visit everyone's house on Christmas, and how that could affect a child's spirit.

During my formative years, I was sheltered from the reality that many families did not have what we had. I got spoiled in my grandparents' world. My tenth year, however, my life changed. That year at Christmas, both of my grandparents were gone. They had died in close proximity, both in their early sixties: Nan from cancer, and Granddad from a broken heart. Although everyone did their best to make Christmas magic, no one could recreate the sparkle of Nan and Granddad.

My memories remain close to this day. I always felt as though I was my grandfather's most special treasure; and Nan, well, she made everyone feel special. I remember when just the two of us were home alone, sitting at her kitchen table and eating cream straight from the carton, the thick, whipped variety well known in England for topping pies and trifles. We dipped our spoons into the carton and laughed till our sides burst! The first Christmas without my grandparents, I cried for everything I had lost.

Not long after my grandparents passed, I got to choose a kitten to bring home for the family, a cute brown-and-white one. My little sister wanted desperately to call her Mangus, but my brother and I won the vote; her name was Pippa. She became a bridge to help us adjust to the loss we felt in our lives now that our grandparents were gone. I missed them a lot, but with just one stroke of my hand on the soft fur of a kitten, I was reminded of the unconditional love they had brought into my world.

My early teen years were filled with dance lessons, school, and my first Saturday job. By my late teens, I had become an independent young woman who didn't want to march to the same beat as my peers. I started to see a pattern in the world around me. All the faces remained the same. I watched as girls got married to the boyfriends they had dated in school and had babies. Kids having kids. Some changed partners, but it was always the same local faces doing the same things. The professions they chose were never surprising; they either knew a friend or assumed a parent's role.

But not me. I was yearning to meet new people, people who were willing to venture out of their comfort zones. I was heeding that little voice within, calling me to adventure. I still believed in my grandparents' loving world where I was everything and could do anything I dreamed of. I wanted to be an active participant in creating a new destiny for myself. I realized it was up to me. I couldn't wait around for my life to begin. I had to give *myself* the chance to become *myself*—to make my life my own.

The Third Law of Karma: Humility

Listen to the Call of Something Greater—When It Feels Meant to Be, Say Yes

Surrender

I've always had fur and four legs, every time I've come back to this wonderful planet, but I'm not sure exactly why that is. Perhaps in a future lifetime, I will return as a beautifully naked and vulnerable human. But then I'd have to navigate that thing two-legged people talk about that shrouds the simplicity of truth, the thing they call the ego.

If I were human, I might be torn between emulating my current beloved Homo sapiens family or gravitating toward those gentle people Jake is always talking about. Jake has been my best friend for almost seven years now. His personality is so much calmer and more reserved than mine. Often, I'll run circles around him to show how much spunkier my Maltese/shih tzu legs are than his taller, more majestic chocolate Labrador retriever limbs. Truth be told, even back when he was able to run faster than me, he never did.

I think he's just too sweet to shatter my illusion that we are on equal footing.

I was a puppy when Jake first told me about the red-robed monks who chant and meditate day in and day out. It seems like an easygoing life. They just keep busy *being*, kind of like me and Jake, no matter what's going on around them. They don't brag about how this one has the most colorful robe and that one sings the loudest. They're what Jake called "humble." In fact, he told me about them to help me understand that word, along with "ego." Jake's taught me an awful lot.

And I know the monks are special people. They remind me of palm trees. I've noticed that even in the harshest storms, a palm tree's trunk does not break but only bends in the wind. The same is true for these monks. They don't get caught up in the storms around them either. That might be part of how they stay humble. They don't pay much attention to the trappings of wealth and prestige; they don't need a golden bowl when earthenware will do. They don't fight to try to create a life just as they pictured it, down to the last detail. Instead they stay centered and quiet, and I think that must make it easier for them to know what's right and true.

If I were human, I'm not sure which road I

would take: the one that puts my ego in charge or the one the monks have chosen. But it's fun to think about monks as I snuggle up with Nicki. And I am happy to sit quietly and wait for my favorite human to tell me what we'll do next.

Sowing the Seeds of Adventure

Many parents fuss over their children leaving the nest, but my parents were not among them. My siblings and I were taught the roots of responsibility while always being encouraged to make use of our wings of independence.

At the age of eighteen my brother was installing glass windows on buildings as far away as Saudi Arabia. By the age of twenty he was back on English soil and getting married, just like everyone else I knew at that age. For most young people in Bromley, finishing the second decade of life meant it was time to settle down.

As for me, being a homemaker didn't line up. Some awkward dates came and went—sometimes not fast enough. If he showed up with too much enthusiasm, I looked for the odd excuse to cut out early.

I preferred to hang out at pubs with guys who were easy to be around, my brother's friends. They were always up for a game of darts, and I was good at the game. The girls in the group could be nasty. They were definitely less laid back and actually more competitive. Sex, marriage, and children were the endgame in the back of most girls' minds. To me, the patterns of their lives felt closed down. Try as I might, I could never fit into that box.

My road to committed love got off to a bad start. I had my first serious boyfriend, Peter, at age fifteen. In retrospect, he was a very poor choice for me. After almost six months invested in our relationship and just days before my sixteenth birthday, he mercilessly dumped me to go back to his old girlfriend. It was a stinging slap to my young ego.

Then there was the night of the big house party. When it wound to a close, there were no cabs available. Those who stayed behind were scattered about the house, passed out on chairs and too drunk to drive. I'd been drinking too.

The bedroom was dark, except for the streetlight that shined through a window, allowing me to see the face of a guy who entered the room shortly after I had settled in. There were two beds in the room, so it was pretty clear what his intention was when he got into mine. Yet I found myself unable to move or even speak as he approached me. He got on top of me. I contemplated shouting, pushing him away, and pictured the scene that would cause. What would the other girls—all experienced sexually when I wasn't—think of me? I knew they would laugh at me, at a minimum. I'd seen how cruel they could be when they didn't think some girl was up to their standards of cool.

Within minutes, it was over. He lifted his weight off me and left. I hadn't put up a fight; he wasn't a stranger—he was someone I knew. Peter's older brother!

I lay there and pretended it wasn't so bad. All the while I wondered why he had felt entitled to do what he did. Was he trying to outscore his brother? Was I doing that too, in some twisted, messed-up way, and why hadn't I stopped him?

He had left the room rather proud of himself while I was left alone. That night tipped the scales of life for me. I moved toward a new social direction: playing it safe.

I found myself spending time with my friend Janet and her husband, who lived between Bromley and London. Janet loved me for me. She was a little older than the crowd I'd been running around with, and being with her made it easy to grow past that phase of my life. Saturday nights and

Sunday roasts—the laughter never ended with her and her family. I felt safe, away from the teenage pressures for a while. That is, until I met Simon.

Simon was a handsome, fair-skinned English lad with a head of thick, brown, wavy hair. We met at work, and on our first date I watched him play in a squash tournament. He won the game, and afterward we went to an Indian restaurant. Simon had tremendous skill on the squash court, and I admired his strength and agility. I quickly became attracted to his gentle nature and the sweet way he respected his mother. I jumped at every opportunity to be in his company. For a time there, I worshipped the ground he walked on. I'd do anything for his approval. All the while, I was never really sure if the admiration was mutual.

Our on-again, off-again dates never got serious. I later learned that a friend of Simon's had warned him that I would trap him into marriage if I could, and he responded by keeping up his guard. It wasn't true—I wasn't ready to think about marriage, though I would have given the relationship a real chance—and his keeping himself at a distance hurt a lot at the time. But it turned out to be a gift, another pivotal point in my life. His aimlessness left an opening for me to set my own direction.

I was independent. I worked hard and owned my own car. I was ready for that day when things finally got a whole lot more interesting.

. . .

Arlene was an American I met at the squash club in the summer of 1980. She was never afraid to say what was on her mind and was different from anyone I had known. She looked amazing with her cool fashion sense: a leather jacket with leggings and matching boots and bag. Her brightly colored designer jumpers always matched her scarf and belt; she absolutely adored shopping in the West End of London. Her tanned, petite frame stood out in a crowd, and her American accent and confidence were utterly captivating to me. She was direct—she asked questions continually, unlike English ladies, who did their best to be polite and quiet. Arlene was confident, not rude, soft spoken yet strong and forward. Because she came from a culture that was bringing women onto equal footing with men, she wasn't afraid to speak up. I enjoyed her immensely.

Arlene constantly questioned why she didn't see a healthy lifestyle trend in England. Walking and running by the ocean on Laguna Beach were second nature to her own lifestyle. Going to the gym was a daily activity when she'd lived in California. Now far from her roots, she was living in Bromley on Westmoreland Road, with her daughter and her new English boyfriend. Her third-floor flat was as fashionable as she was. It was furnished in a brightly colored, modern style I'd never seen in any traditional English home.

I remember well driving out to visit Arlene on one unusually hot afternoon. The sweltering, dry air poured in through my open window as I drove to her flat. When I got there, Arlene's daughter, Mia, opened the door wearing her mother's smile and pointed toward the kitchen, where Arlene spent most of her time when she was at home. Arlene was preparing Spanish-style steaks. She always made dinner from scratch, but to me it looked like way too much work.

"Why aren't you having dinner with Simon tonight?" she asked.

"Why is it so hard to find the kind of relationship I want?" I countered.

Arlene let that one go—she knew I wasn't really looking to her for an answer right then. "I went to Covent Garden today for peanut butter," she said as she sliced green peppers. Arlene had told me she found it provincial that the only bell peppers she could find in our town were green.

"Seriously?! London for peanut butter!" I asked.

"That's what the fella at the grocery store thought too."

"Well, it is a two-hour drive, round-trip," I replied.

"Nicki, why is everyone so content to have boundaries here? It feels so strange to me that people don't want to get out and explore."

"What do you mean?"

"How can you grow if you don't venture out? Although I must say, he was a very funny bloke, that fella today." Arlene shrugged and gave her impersonation of a Cockney accent. "*Blimey, Luv, nuffin' 'ere ya fancy? And there's you goin' all the way to Timbukfree. Long way, innit!*"

"He's got that right," I laughed. "The last time I made the trip to London, it was with you because I won't even drive into the city myself."

"You mean when I brought you to that fancy club with the great long bar?" she asked.

"Yup, that's the time. I'd never been to a London nightclub before," I smiled.

Just then, Arlene's teenage daughter walked into the kitchen, wearing a miniskirt and a T-shirt covered with colorful fish. Her long brown hair had blonde highlights from the California sun, and her complexion was so perfect that she glowed.

"Mia looks like a model, Arlene. What are you feeding her?" I blurted out.

"Teenagers around here are not toned enough in my opinion. We make sure we eat well and exercise regularly so our muscles stay in shape."

"I'm thinking that might be easier to do in California, on the beach and surfing the ocean waves. Here in Bromley, we don't seem to have as much opportunity for the kind of activity you're used to," I replied.

I enjoyed listening to Arlene's stories about California. Before I met her, America to me was just Walt Disney and *Miami Vice* on TV. She made California sound so incredible. I couldn't understand why she hadn't moved back there with her daughter and new boyfriend. Why was she here?

"Arlene, what do you like about living in England?" I asked.

"Hmmm. Well, I'd have to say that I dig the camaraderie you Brits have for one another. Your sense of humor cracks me up, the way you make fun of each other and laugh about it. In the US, we tend to take ourselves way too seriously, although I have to admit sometimes I fall for it when the joke is on me!"

She put together some final ingredients while I thought about what she had said. We did make fun of ourselves and share great laughs at each other's expense. I didn't realize back then that my dry sense of humor wasn't universal. I started back in with my questions.

"What do you miss about California, other than your peanut butter and jelly sandwiches?" I laughed.

"Well, right now," she said, her expression earnest, "I miss the vegetables. In England they either serve you green beans or brussels sprouts. Blah. I like a variety of veggies."

We moved to the living room, and I sat on the white carpet with my back against the blue sofa.

"What are you homesick for?" I continued.

"Mexican tortillas from Laguna Beach. And oh, what I wouldn't do for some homemade guacamole right now!" she complained.

I rolled into a belly laugh. Sweet Arlene, always so honest, so serious, and ready to answer all my questions. "What's so funny?" she asked.

"Oh, I don't know, maybe it's that British humor kicking in, but if I were homesick for something, I can tell you right now, it would not be for fruits and vegetables!" We both laughed this time. "Maybe a cream slice and a cup of tea, but definitely not fruits and vegetables," I repeated.

Once the laughter ebbed, Arlene looked long-ingly out the window. She took a deep breath in and then softly said, "What I really miss is the smell of the Pacific Ocean with its seaweed and salt air."

I didn't realize it at the time, but in that moment the seeds of an American life were being lovingly planted in my subconscious. I took to Arlene's kindness like a bee to a flower and was inspired by every story she shared. I hung out with her as often as I could and did my best to support her through some of the challenges of being in a new country, with new relationships. She was an *American girl*, with an open and feminist personality, and I could listen to her talk about America all day long.

By the summer of 1982, Arlene finally did return to California, and I slipped back into my predictable English routine—until the moment when everything changed.

. . .

It was just another day to play squash and then head over to my favorite Indian restaurant.

I was in the club's changing room after my lesson when I overheard a conversation between two women, one of whom I recognized. Catherine was consoling her friend Jane, who had just failed a nursing exam. She would have to take it again, and was now unable to go on the vacation they had planned—a trip to America. I listened as they discussed who could take Jane's place. My whole body raced with excitement as I tried to look casual and tune in to what they were saying. Catherine was running out of options; she didn't have any other friends who could take a month off to travel to America. Without a second thought, I joined their conversation.

"America? Where in America? I could be interested in something like that," I chirped with excitement that was almost impossible to contain. Catherine had lined up a vacation property perched on the Gulf of Mexico. A beautiful two-bedroom condo named The Gulfview on Marco Island in Florida.

Have you ever just known instantly that something was meant for you? That drop-everything-because-your-ship-has-arrived feeling? This was *my* moment. Catherine explained some of the details with enthusiasm and within minutes—yes, just minutes—I told her I was in! I would spend a month on some island I had never heard of before, with a woman I hardly knew.

With an open heart and mind, I would accept Catherine's invitation to visit America and change my fate. All I knew was that the door to the Land of Opportunity stood wide open, giving me clear direction that sometimes when we get out of our own way, we create the space to heed a wiser voice.

The Fourth Law of Karma: Growth

When We Change Ourselves,
Our Lives Change Too

Act from your inner truth

Heavy eyelids overtake me as I lie on my chair and watch a light rain fall outside. A tropical storm came by this morning—it was *crashing down!*—and now the golf course is flooded. I won't be able to walk with Jake today. I can almost see his home across the green, and I wonder if he is watching the rain taper off too.

The soft sound of the warm shower on the windowpane is soothing. It makes me think about who I am and why I'm here. I know my purpose and passion right now is to help Nicki sort out the years leading up to leaving England for America on her quest for growth.

The law of growth states that we create our own opportunities through the choices we make. If we keep making the same choices, we'll keep getting the same results, good or bad. I'm exceptionally grateful Nicki chose to come to this place. It's truly a piece of paradise, and I'm without a doubt one of the luckiest dogs on this planet.

Yesterday, Jake came for a visit and we went for a walk together. He can't see as well as he once did, and he doesn't walk as far anymore, but he always knows my house and how to find me. Who needs perfect sight when you have a canine nose, right? When I'm with him, it's easy to remember the first lesson he taught me when I was young: *wherever you go, there you are.* So simple, right? Back then I thought he was talking about our walks. Now I know he was talking about our thoughts.

Dreaming of Paradise

It was my twenty-first birthday. Simon's older brother had insisted on throwing me a big party. "Everyone needs a party when they turn twenty-one," he said.

It was hard to argue with that. "All right," I agreed. "Let's go crazy!"

But it was pretty hard to capture my attention that night. My thoughts were a million miles away. Or, to be more precise, 4,488 miles away. Details of our trip to Marco Island just kept playing through my mind. *First get a month off work. Second, book my flights.* Catherine and I would be spending all of November on Marco. It was nearly three months away, but I was ready to get on a plane *now*.

The party was a milestone to remember. Everyone had a good time. A song by Lionel Richie came on, "Once, Twice, Three Times a Lady." I hadn't seen Simon for a while, which was nothing unusual for us. He swooped over to me as though no time had passed, took my hand, and asked me to dance. "This is your song," he said.

Then came the questions about my upcoming trip.

"So, I hear you're going to America with that Catherine person from the squash club?"

I started to describe all the things I needed to sort out and all the plans Catherine and I had already made. I hardly let Simon get a word in edgewise.

"Something is different about you tonight," he said.

I stopped talking, thinking I was saying too much, that I tended to waffle on. Taking a breath, I looked into his eyes. I felt different. For the first time, I felt like I was looking straight through him. Instead of trying to appease him or explain the shift I was feeling, I just smiled and continued dancing until the last note was done. Within my moment of quiet with Simon, my need for his approval began to fade. Then a new song was playing—Rod Stewart this time, singing "You're in My Heart"—and this rowdy bunch burst into the chorus together, most of us out of tune but we had heart, soul, and every other word down.

All except for Simon, who took a seat at the bar and looked on.

We laughed and sang, and I was able to honor everything I had always been. But the talks I had shared with Arlene had blossomed, and I was ready for the next chapter in my life.

To America

As we boarded our flight, all the hype and worries melted away. In their place came a calmer form of emotion that I could only describe as . . . anticipation. Once you sit in your seat and the engines whirl to a roar, there's really nothing left to do but sit back and enjoy the ride.

I looked around at the other people on the plane. Most were much older than Catherine and me. Some were in business suits and some dressed in smart, fashionable styles. But we were casual and ready for a long flight aboard TWA. Catherine turned to me, smiling from ear to ear.

"Thank you so much for showing up that day at the squash club," she said. "We're going to have such a splendid time. You're going to love this place!"

I sipped on the drink the stewardess

brought me. I had ordered a martini and lemonade, a spritzer-like drink common in the pubs in Bromley. The American stewardess had returned with a gin martini in one hand and a lemon drink in the other. It was the start of my education in a whole new language—and a new way of life.

"I am going to love it," I said to Catherine.

It felt like an enchanted moment, like in *Peter Pan* when Wendy is about to leap above the snowy rooftops of London to fly past Big Ben and off to some island paradise. A place to swim with creatures of the sea, a place where absolutely anything is possible. I closed my eyes and fell asleep.

. . .

When our plane landed in Florida, the first thing I saw were the palm trees, more than I had imagined, rows and rows of them along the roads, standing tall along the medians, dividing traffic. The hot sun in November felt good, but the rental car felt strange with its steering wheel on the left side. We drove out of Miami and entered the Everglades, traveling through every major natural habitat in the region: fire-shaped pinelands, saw grass marshes, cypress domes, sloughs, alligators swimming in waterways beside the road. After two hours, we finally saw a bridge up ahead.

We topped the rise of the bridge and for the first time, the picture-perfect postcard I'd only seen in a travel brochure was now coming to life. We found ourselves entering a tropical oasis. Home to one of the largest mangrove forests in the world, the island was surrounded by sparkling water the color of emeralds and sand beaches as soft as white sugar.

When we checked into our Gulfview condo, a security guard verified our names on the registry and then let us in through the automatic glass doors. The elevator stopped at our floor, and when I opened the door to our condo, I could see the sun setting over the ocean. In the kitchen stood the largest fridge I had ever seen, and each bedroom sported a California king-size bed. I'd never seen a bed so huge! I threw myself onto it, my arms outstretched, and laughed out loud.

Decorated with designer tastes, all the rooms were connected by a yellow and green colored theme, so different from the homes in England where rooms each had completely different décor.

"I feel like Rod Stewart's girlfriend, and I could live like this forever!" I called out.

"I know—it's so perfect here!" Catherine shouted back from the balcony. "I told you so."

To be thrilled about this way of life was easy, but there was something much deeper happening. For me, it was more the natural state of gratitude I felt while I was there. I would think, Wow, this is so special, what an honor. Why me?

I loved every second of what Catherine and I did that month. Picnics on the beach, celebration dinners in Naples. I even found that going to the supermarket was a treat. The cashiers would greet you and I would thank them and offer to pack my own bag.

"Let me help. In England no one packs our bags for us," I would say.

She would have none of it. "We do it for you here, hon'." And she would continue to pack my groceries and tell me to have a nice day.

On Marco Island in the 1980s, young people spent the days soaking up the sun's rays on the beach and the nights working at local restaurants. It was casual, and the people were laid back. Island-style living in this fishing community managed to "live and let live," with a promise of change that really called to me.

Catherine and I had left behind our leggings and boots, and instead sat on pristine beaches in new bikinis. In England, you would have to wait in long lines for just about everything. But not here—service was first class in America. All you had to do was pick up the phone and place an order for what you wanted, even a new bed! Order it one day and have it delivered the next.

Proper identification was a big deal here too. In the pubs in England you could drink at age eighteen, but in the US you had to be twenty-one to buy a drink. Then there was my obsession with getting an American driver's license, which was a novelty at first—I wanted to have it as a souvenir to take home. It was ridiculously fast and easy to get a license compared to back home. You showed up and took the test, and then it was yours. The manual gears I used in my car in England had been replaced with an automatic transmission in my rental car. The roads were straight and so easy to navigate.

All that I had hoped for presented itself to me during this month of bliss. I suppose I could have chalked it up to an unrealistic way of life

that is only available to a select few. That, however, was the furthest thing from my thoughts.
To me, what I saw was a community of people
who followed their passions to the fullest, while
allowing others around them to do the same.

Within the circle of people I had the privilege
to meet, I sensed a level of acceptance that signaled more choices, more growth, and a new
way of life. As our trip came to an end, Catherine
and I stopped at the largest restaurant on the island. They told us they were hiring for their busy
season in February, and February was only two
months away. We were definitely interested. I
knew it would be senseless for me to resist the
pull of America. I had changed inside, and now a
whole new life was rushing up to greet me. Even
at twenty-one, I was beginning to understand
that *when our inner world changes, the outer
world will answer the call.*

. . .

We buckled up our seat belts for the ride home.
The plane was full, and so were we—full of
ideas, that is. If we were going to take this leap,
we would need to plan for it right away, before
we got settled back into our predictable routines.

We couldn't let this experience become some faded memory of a once-upon-a-time dream.

. . .

A flight attendant announced we were to remain in our seats as we touched down at London's Heathrow airport. Our eight-hour flight was over. I was about to share my news of the exciting new chapter of my life with my mum and dad. But the lump in my throat and the tears trailing down my cheeks told another story: how hard it would be to leave this place behind—my parents, England, the comforts of the life I'd grown up with.

I took a deep breath and dabbed at my face with my sleeve. My heart had made its choice. Now wasn't the time for tears, or fears, or the thought, What *if it all goes wrong?*

Part 2—Fire and Fur

How people treat you is their karma;
how you react is yours.
—Wayne Dyer

The Fifth Law of Karma: Responsibility

Our Lives Are a Result of Our Actions

Manifest the life you dream

Once in canine training class, Jake and I watched together as our humans tried out a new technique with us called the mirror method. The main idea of that lesson was that everything we canines do is up to our humans; we simply mirror back what they are doing. So if our humans aren't getting the response they're looking for from us, they need to look more closely at what they are doing to produce that outcome. We dogs reflect what the humans are feeling and thinking and accomplishing.

I asked Jake, "I know this is supposed to be canine training, but isn't this reflecting business more of an issue that our humans need to work on?"

"Oh, yes, Karma," Jake replied in his deep, wise voice. "This is definitely about our humans, and I once heard it said that humans do not see the world as it is. They see it as they are."

Jake continued. "Let me tell you a Sufi parable

I've heard that explains things nicely, and this one has been passed down through the ages."

For a moment, my tail does figure eights. I sit down, get comfortable, my ears perked forward and my head cocked to one side. "Yes, Jake."

"The story starts out with a stranger who enters a village," Jake begins. "Immediately, he looks for the village's Sufi master to ask his advice. The stranger says, 'I'm thinking of moving to this village. What can you tell me about the people who reside here?'

"The Sufi master replies, 'What can you tell me about the people who live where you come from?'

"The visitor frowns, and color comes to his cheeks. 'Ah,' he says angrily. 'That's why I left my town. There are terrible people there—robbers, cheats, and liars! They stab each other in the back all the time.'"

Wow, I thought, this all sounds very bad! I sat up a little straighter as Jake continued.

"'Well, now,' says the Sufi master. 'Isn't that a coincidence? That's exactly what people are like here.' Disappointed—no, more like disgusted—the man then departs the village and is never seen again.

"Soon, another stranger enters the village, and he too seeks out the Sufi master for advice.

The stranger says, 'I'm thinking of coming to live in this village. What can you tell me about the people who live here?'

"The Sufi master replies as before: 'What can you tell me about the people who live where you come from?'

"'Ah,' says the visitor in fond remembrance, 'they are wonderful people. They're kind, gentle, and compassionate. They look after each other.'

"'Well now,' says the Sufi master, 'isn't that a coincidence? That's exactly what the townspeople are like here too.'

"So you see, Karma," Jake said, "this story tells us that humans take their inner selves with them wherever they go, and whatever they believe on the inside, they see reflected in the world. That means that their world can only be changed from within.

"They must learn to take responsibility for their circumstances and discover that our love will mirror what's in their hearts."

Returning to Marco

It was February 3, 1983, when Catherine and I landed in America for the second time. An immigration officer, a kind fellow, took our passports and asked the purpose of our visit.

"Traveling to Miami to see friends, then off to Marco Island," I explained. "Then we're thinking we might drive to California before we return home." I had no idea of the vast distances between Florida and the West Coast—nothing was that far away in England.

"That will take you a while. Need to sell a few pizzas along the way, no doubt," he remarked with a grin. I wondered what he would ask us next, but he had no more questions for us. He stamped our passports, and we moved on through customs.

Preparing to go back to America the second time had been an entirely different experience from the first. My vacation mind-set was a thing of the past; I was starting a different kind of journey. I had cleaned out my life of twenty-one years, selling my car and packing up everything I could fit into a suitcase. I had made sure to pack two English treasures in particular both small, fine bone china dishes: one Staffordshire with purple forget-me-nots painted around the edge, and the other Royal Grafton with three gorgeous butterflies, one of which was named the American Lady. I had carefully tucked the pieces of china between my clothes.

Some treasured items needed to stay behind because they were too big, like the pineapple glass that once belonged to my nan and my record player. Oh, how I wanted to take my music with me! Music that was such a huge part of my world while I was growing up. Once settled in my seat on the plane, I could still see in my mind the turntable spinning for the last time, the arm and needle moving across the vinyl LP and the rich sound of Diana Ross singing, "It's myyyy turn just for me." It was my turn—my real shot at the American dream.

Watching the cold, gray, rainy days of England disappear over the Atlantic Ocean, I felt more of a sense of the separation between my old and new worlds this time. And when the officer stamped our passports as we entered the country, I didn't know how long this new adventure would last, whether I would get homesick and quickly return. But something deep down told me I had just taken the biggest step of my life.

. . .

The first couple of weeks we slept on floors; friends of friends of Catherine's allowed us to stay with them in Miami. By the middle of February, we had made our way back to Marco Island. We moved into an apartment fit for a movie star (at least I thought so), and in a few months' time, when the busy snowbird season was over, we would travel. It was all fun for me, even the work.

The first three months were so busy that I didn't think about England much. At least not until Simon's sister-in-law wrote to me. She wanted to tell me that Simon was looking forward to visiting me, that he had hopes for our relationship. She had an added message—another woman was pushing hard to get Simon's ring and I'd better call him fast! My old longing for a storybook relationship with Simon flooded back, and I desperately wanted to pick up the phone right away. But I was torn. I knew I had to follow my dream, and I didn't see how Simon could ever be a part of it. I eventually did call, but only to let him know that

I would be traveling with Catherine on the dates when he was planning to visit and that I wasn't sure when I would return.

Talking with Simon felt like going back in time. I pictured him clearly on the night of my birthday party, reaching his arm across the table to pull me to the dance floor. For the first time ever, he hadn't been in a hurry to leave. We had both changed, and now I had new confidence and a sense of who I was without him. He'd touched the flower in the vase at the center of the table. "I missed more opportunities than I want to think of right now," he'd said. "I never even sent you flowers."

It had been an awkward moment. Simon had never shown such a serious side before, and now, talking with him on the phone on this night, the last thing I wanted was to give him the invitation to open that door again. Before I hung up, I told Simon I would call when I returned from our road trip. I think he knew that I wasn't going to—and I didn't. It was time for us both to move on.

. . .

Catherine and I flew to Colorado, rented a car, and drove through the lowland meadows and aspen groves of the Rockies. When I had passed my driver's test back in England, taking that first ride up Swan Hill on my own had been a nerve-racking journey. It wasn't easy to finesse the clutch control on a slope in traffic without experience. Now in Colorado, my driving dexterity was being tested again. Driving through the mountains was thrilling at every turn, and the higher we climbed, the more my nerves went into overdrive. I could feel my blood pumping through my veins—this was no Swan Hill! I was in suspense on every nail-biting corner.

Colorado was spectacular, and it wasn't until that leg of our travels that we realized how big the US was and how unrealistic it would be for us to see everything we had in mind—including California—which seemed too far west now. A stunning boat ride on Lake Mead was our final highlight for the Centennial State. We then shifted gears, flying back home to Marco only to hit the road again up the eastern seaboard.

Washington, DC, was a stop en route. We took plenty of pictures at several historical sites, including the Lincoln Memorial and the White House, before finding our way to the Big Apple. New York was an entirely different experience from Marco Island or Colorado. I found the security systems extreme and disconcerting, with the triple-bolts on the doors, echoing down the stairways when they slid into place. A busy metropolis that truly never sleeps, New York City was in direct contrast to Marco Island. Like the yin to its yang.

Once we got to Upstate New York, we met two fun-loving Canadian girls with almost identical names, Jen and Jenny. They were heading home to Niagara Falls, high on our list of places to see.

Crossing the border into Canada was the best way to spend a day to cure some English cravings. The people were so friendly, and the goodies we missed from back home were everywhere. Biscuits, like my favorite thick, rich shortbread from Scotland, with an English cup of tea. To top it all off, we had a cream slice with real cream! I had missed these velvety tastes I grew up with in England. By late afternoon, we had found an English pub, where we played a game of darts and ordered a plate of fish with piping hot chips straight out of the fryer, smothered in salt and vinegar. We thoroughly enjoyed the smells and tastes of home.

Niagara Falls was definitely worthy of being called a natural wonder of the world. The thundering roar of aqua-green water, the rising mist relentlessly spilling over the edge of the falls—it was breathtaking. It would be an understatement to say that we had a great day; it was amazing—until we tried to get back over the border into the United States.

The American border patrol officer was not nearly as accommodating as the fellow who had stamped our passports when we first arrived in the US. This time we were met by a short, stocky man who was possibly one of the most unpleasant souls I had ever encountered in my life. He seemed angry at the world, and it soon became clear that whatever had gone wrong with his day, he was going to take out on us.

He took Catherine into a small white cement-block room with fluorescent lighting and demanded that she empty her bag onto a table. All I had with me were a pocketbook, loose change, and my passport, but Catherine had much more, including her diary and all her plans for everyone she wanted to see.

After he escorted Catherine back to the car and handed us both our passports, he asked, "Can you explain why you came to the United States on a one-way ticket?"

I couldn't come up with a convincing response. We had shown him our passports and visas. It was obvious his mind was made up, and every time Catherine tried to explain, he interrupted her and called her a liar. It was an awful experience, but the truth was, we couldn't provide any proof of when we would return to England. I, for one, didn't plan to yet.

Glaring at us all the while, the officer smugly announced, "I'm going to personally see to it that you never set foot on American soil again!"

We then had to drive back over the bridge to deal with the Canadian border patrol. It all seemed very harsh to me.

Suddenly, I had this crazy thought. What would happen if I got stuck on this bridge and I couldn't get back into either country? We approached a Canadian officer who, thankfully, advised us to go to the English consulate first thing in the morning and sort out what to do next. He wished us well and waved us on.

It was time for a new plan. We had so many belongings in Florida. I wanted my bone china, my American Lady butterfly dish. Was it possible I'd have to leave everything behind?

We stayed at a B and B and met up with Jen and Jenny the next morning. We had a major problem on our hands, and these generous girls were willing to help us in any way they could. We were stressed. Overnight, I suffered a migraine headache, and Catherine literally broke out in shingles. She tossed and turned in agony all night long while I analyzed every possible scenario for how this situation would play out. *Will we finish this adventure in Canada? It certainly might be an option.*

I heard those same awful words over and over again in my head: "*I'm going to personally see to it that you never set foot on American soil again!*" They only made me feel more determined. *My life is my responsibility now,* I realized. I had a crystal-clear idea of what I wanted. I hadn't come this far only to give up on that dream.

As I mulled over my options, another situation weighed heavily on my mind as well. My parents would be arriving to visit me on Marco Island very soon. This presented a problem. International communication was much more difficult in those days, and contacting my parents since I'd left home had consisted of a monthly call from a pay phone and postcards every so often to show them where I'd been. I would have to figure out a way to get back to Florida before they arrived.

We decided to hold off on going to the consulate. Instead, we would try again to cross the border on our own. It wasn't the best idea for Catherine's shingles, but she went with it, in spite of the pain.

When we arrived there, many people were walking across the bridge leading to America. We decided to stay close behind a man and a woman with two young children the whole way; the plan was to walk through with them as one big happy family. But when we reached the border, an officer stopped us dead in our tracks, saying, "Just a minute, girls! Show me your passports."

We handed them over without a word.

He studied them for a minute, went inside his cubby hole, and returned with bad news: "I can't let you through."

The family we'd been trying to attach ourselves to had been waved on, so I instantly knew we were in trouble. But there *had* to be a way to convince this man to let us return. I tried to explain what had happened the day before, but it was a waste of effort.

"I'm very sorry, ladies," he said. "What happened yesterday, that was really bad luck. But I still can't let you through."

"Couldn't I just put my toe on that side of the border for a moment?" I asked, wanting so badly to touch American soil again.

"Sorry, miss, but I can't let you. If you had come to me today without yesterday's encounter, you would be in the US right now. It's unfortunate, but you're going to have to sort it out from the other side."

We trudged back over to Canada, and I looked back toward the bridge that now stood between me and my dream. I knew that getting across it or not would determine the direction of the rest of my life.

. . .

After a good night's rest and a plan to be third-time lucky, we decided to give it one last go. Jen seemed to think it might be easier to get across at night, which was a super busy time at the border, especially on a weekend, which this happened to be. The bridge filled up with cars as young Canadians crossed the border to exchange the Ontario scene, where last call came at midnight, for the bars in Buffalo, which were open until two.

"You can show your driver's license if they ask for identification," Jen suggested. "That's all they ask for when they're busy on the bridge."

Catherine and I practiced our Canadian accents all day. Around midnight, we got into our friends' car, and they drove us toward the border. As we approached, Catherine spotted a border patrol officer and gasped. "Bloody 'ell!" she said, "It's him, it's him!"

She was looking at a patrol officer who was talking to someone in the car just in front of us. I peered ahead. I didn't think it was the grumpy guard, but Catherine was so stressed that there was no convincing her otherwise. Maybe I'd had more margaritas throughout the evening than she'd had, but I was remarkably relaxed. A sense of calm washed over me as I focused on thoughts of being back in our beautiful apartment on Marco Island. When we got up to the kiosk, the officer leaned down and looked at each of us in turn. "I'll need to see identification from all of you, ladies," he said. While our driver, Jenny, was rummaging in her purse, I showed him my Florida license, which I had only gotten on a whim, just because it was so much easier to do than it was in England, plus I could.

"Not Canadian," he said, glancing at me again. No matter how much we had practiced our Canadian accents in the pub earlier, they were no good to us now.

"No," I replied, passport in hand. "Just visiting."

"Me too," Catherine said. She showed him her ID.

"Where are you headed, ladies?"

"Just across into the States to enjoy the night-life," Jenny said as she held out her license.

"Don't know why the pubs close so early here," Jen chimed in from the passenger's seat. She was the last to flash her ID.

"Well enjoy yourselves then," the officer said. And then he waved us through. Just like that!

Our wait wasn't over yet, though; the bridge was jam packed, and it seemed to take forever to reach the sign that declared, ENTERING THE UNITED STATES.

. . .

Reflecting on my actions as that young, determined woman, I know I was naïve. I didn't fully grasp the legal repercussions that might result from my choices, or how close I'd come to having to return to family in England with only the stain of failure to show for my American adventure. But I was willing to act, and overcome my fears in order to do so. My inner vision was such a clear beacon guiding me to reflect and manifest that vision in the outer world. And I knew that *the responsibility for realizing my dream lay squarely in my own young hands.*

The Sixth Law of Karma: Connection

Everything Serves an Equal Purpose

There are no accidents

I've been training a new dog-sitter for the past couple of weeks. She's a lovely young human named Greta who wears Lululemon yoga clothes every day and enjoys taking me for long walks and talks. Seriously, she speaks to me like I'm a human the whole time we're together.

Sadly, I don't think things are going to work out for Greta to continue to dog-sit on Marco. She and her husband are going through a challenging divorce, and now she might be moving away. But somehow it doesn't seem to get her down. Greta has a great way of seeing life and saying the nicest things.

"Karma, I know we were meant to spend some time with each other for a reason. Every day, life is just a series of meaningful coincidences."

Greta is right: there are no accidents. Every step we take leads to the next and is just as important as the last. Our past, our present, and our future are all connected, just as everyone and everything in this universe is connected. The only way to find and appreciate that connection is to be consciously aware of it. Every relationship we have serves a purpose.

Isn't that a wonderful way to see things? Just one conversation can change how you feel when somebody new crosses your path. When the mail came today, there was a different carrier than the one who usually brings Nicki those piles of paper. I wagged especially hard, so my whole backend wiggled and wobbled, and that made her smile. We were connected! And I bet she passed that smile along to the people next door.

Just last week Greta was dog-sitting Jake when she noticed a small lump on his nose that had started to grow. "Have you taken Jake to his vet to have that looked at?" she asked Jake's human. "It may be nothing, but if it is something, you'd want to get on it early." I call that a *relationship synchronicity*. Whether they're long relationships or short, good or bad, *there are no accidents* when people come into our lives.

I will really miss Greta if she has to go away. Here's something else she said when we were walking and talking.

"Karma, since there are no accidents, it can be helpful to think about what purpose someone else might have in your life. You can never really know for sure, but sometimes you can make a pretty good guess. I know your purpose for being in my life is so I can feel loved. And when you can help someone feel that way, you can be a better companion to everyone. You see how it's all connected? I think you crossed my path to remind me to keep my heart open during a difficult time. I love our walks and talks! Don't you?"

I told Greta yes in the best way I know how—with kisses. Greta always helps me see that *all our interactions serve a purpose*, even if they are little things like kisses that make a difference, especially on Jake's poor ol' nose.

Back on the Right Side of the Border

After our Canadian ordeal, Catherine and I went to Buffalo for a few days to meet up with friends from Marco who had come up for the summer to work, leaving Florida's off-season to find the on-season up north.

We met our friend Gabe at his summer job. Gabe was always trying to hatch a plan to figure out how to marry one of us, despite the fact that he was gay. As much as I wanted to stay in America, and even though I was young and brave enough to take some risks, I knew that was not the solution.

Grateful to be back, we shared our border troubles with Gabe.

"We have to make sure nothing like that ever happens again, my dear girls," he said. "Remember what that woman at the Miami immigration office told you, Nicki, when you asked how you could apply for a green card?" He put his hands on his hips and mimicked a Spanish accent, "The only way you can legally stay in A-mer-i-ca is to get married like I did, señorita!"

"That's what she said, all right," I agreed.

"Now look," Gabe said, "I can't save you both, but I can solve this problem for one of you." He went down on one knee and crossed his hands over his heart. "Will one of you beautiful girls make me the happiest boy on earth? Nicki, Catherine? Will one of you marry me?"

Catherine and I burst out laughing. Gabe grinned and stood up. "Well don't say I never offered."

"And it's a very generous offer, Gabe," I said, "but Catherine here has a new man on the horizon down in Marco. Me, I'll stick with my travel visa. At least it will give me enough time to have my parents over for a visit, and to go see Arlene in California."

"Then let's think about a Plan B, Nicki. I think you might like a fellow who's a friend of mine. He's an American, but if you ask me, he has a sarcastic sense of humor like you Brits, and he's working the bar at the yacht club down in Olcott tonight. I could introduce you."

"Okay, sure. Why not?" I replied. The thought of meeting someone who might remind me of home was intriguing. And after what we had just been through, I was open to some fun.

. . .

A guy walked toward the car as we pulled up to the yacht club's employee side door. Gabe leaned over and rolled down my window.

"Hey, Mike, we're heading out for a drink," he called out. "Are you ready to join us?"

Mike had just finished his shift. "You know me, Gabe, I'm always ready to have some fun, especially when there are beautiful ladies involved." He looked straight at me. "I'd like to know how you meet so many lovely girls, my friend! Where did you find this beauty?"

Mike made his way into the back of the car, and I jumped into the conversation.

"Gabe is a good friend from Marco," I said. "It's serious—he's already proposed to me." I chuckled.

"That's true, I did." Gabe laughed.

"Wow! With an accent like that, who can blame you?" Mike said, adding, "Hey, I'm going out for drinks with a limey and her gay boyfriend!"

At the bar, everyone knew Mike; he seemed like the most popular person in town. More friends arrived, and it didn't take long to see why Gabe thought I might like him. Gabe tried to tell a story about the time Mike had to serve drinks to a bus-load of rowdy women bound for a bridal shower, but he cut him short. "Now, Gabe, don't let your mind wander. It's far too small to be let out on its own."

His spirited sarcasm was refreshing, and having drinks at this bar brought back the fun times I used to have in the pubs at home. Mike wasn't in top shape physically as Simon had been, but he had the same kind of charm. He was a really funny person, truly the life of the party, and I found myself attracted to his sense of humor.

If there was one thing I should have been more concerned about, it was the amount of vodka he consumed that night. I did notice that he ordered many drinks. But where I came from, everyone went to the pubs for social gatherings and drinking was part of the fun. I was actually impressed with how much he could drink and still hold his own.

"I'd like to cook you a dinner when I come to Marco in a couple of months," he said, stroking his mustache. "What do you say?"

"If you can cook as well as you entertain, then absolutely!"

. . .

Catherine and I made our way back to Marco Island, but it wasn't long before we went our separate ways. She had made some new friends and started to get quite heavy into the partying scene—smoking clouds of pot and staying up late. So once again, I didn't fit in. The crowd seemed young to me. I moved into a cozy efficiency apartment and bought a scooter. The little apartment was all I could afford, living by myself, but with its kitchenette and Murphy bed, it was adequate. It was definitely different from the apartment I had left to Catherine and her new friends, but worth it to have my own space.

In October, after the yacht club closed for the season, Mike came to Marco Island to work at a local bar. I slowly began to learn more about him—slowly because he hid behind his laughter. I found out that his father was an atrocious alcoholic. I started to see the pain he was hiding with his own drinking. What I didn't know was that I was only seeing a fraction of what he was actually drinking.

The New Year came and went on the island, and the high-occupancy season was in full swing. Everything was new and fun until January 27, when Mike received a call. I watched him walk in circles, tugging at the curled-up phone cord. The conversation was short; he banged the receiver down, and then raised his voice. "I can't believe how much this man has managed to fuck up my life. Now when things are finally going well for me, the bastard has to die!" Mike was angry that he had to leave. Offering no more details than that, he packed up his things and headed for Buffalo.

It was a week later when I finally heard from him again.

"Nicki, the funeral was tough, and my mom's very fragile right now. I'm staying here for a while. Soon it will be spring, and I'll be back at the club in Olcott. But I don't want to stop seeing you. Even though this may seem fast, the way I see it is that, well . . ." He drew a breath. "I think you should marry me. That way, I can at least get the chance to date you!" He let out a short little laugh to ease the tension. Then he paused for a moment and took a deep breath, hoping to hear a favorable reply from my end. But I didn't know what to say.

After a few seconds of dead air, he continued. "Say yes before I lose you to London. I've had a lengthy conversation with my mom about all of this. She can see how good you are for me, and she would be happy to have you stay with us at her house. She even gave me her engagement ring because she would like for you to have it. What do you say, Nicki? Will you marry me?"

Really? Was this what I wanted for myself? Was I ready to marry this guy? We were just friends. There had been no romance between us, and we truly knew very little about each other. At least, I knew very little about him and his past.

But what if he truly was "the one"? How could I ever know if I walked away from the relationship now? I could regret doing so for the rest of my life. So at twenty-two I made what seemed like the best choice at the time—I said yes. I packed up my apartment and turned in the keys to my independent lifestyle. I agreed to fly to Buffalo to see Mike and to meet his mother, Dot, and to accept her ring.

. . .

Dot's nerves were shot; you could tell the instant you looked at her that her life had been filled with challenge. I accidentally dropped my bag on the floor shortly after entering her house, and she almost jumped out of her skin. She was not only easily shaken, but also frail. She was on oxygen, the breathing tube perched beneath her nostrils. I'd never known someone to be in that condition. I'd had no idea what I was walking into.

"You're as pretty as Mike said you were," she half-smiled between gasps for air. "I think he's a very lucky man to have you in his life."

Dot was a kind lady. She made me feel so welcome, and I spent much time with her while Mike worked his afternoon and late evening shifts. A couple of months passed, and she helped plan the wedding. Part of the plan included my signing a prenuptial agreement—for the ring. If our marriage failed, the ring would go back to Dot. As the wedding day approached, I reminded Dot that I still hadn't signed that agreement.

Her expression turned serious. "You don't need to," she said. "He's getting more like his father every day, and that worries me. If this marriage doesn't work out, it won't be your fault."

Shivers ran up my back and across my neck and prickled my hair, but I just shook off the chill and ignored my doubts. I tried to convince myself that Mike didn't have a serious problem. He was just upset about his father; that's why he was drinking so much. I really felt sorry for him—I could tell he was hurting. I didn't know that alcoholics are masters at hiding the truth about their addiction even from the people in their lives who are closest to them. That they can take you along into the spiral of despair. If I had known these things at the time, I would have seen all the signs I needed, right there on Dot's face. Her husband had stripped her of all her courage and confidence. But I was a fearless, strong-minded, young British girl who thought she knew exactly what she was doing.

It is true that there are no accidents, even when we stumble into our darkest hours. In the unconscious spirit of life lessons yet to learn, I married Mike.

The Seventh Law of Karma: Focus

Energy Flows Where Attention Goes

You can choose—
struggle or ease

Water came pouring down from the ceiling a few weeks ago, like a spring rainstorm showing up without warning. This storm, however, was in our kitchen! I could hardly contain myself as I ran in and out of the saturating spray, barking and gliding across the wet floor. I felt like a seal pup on fresh ice for the first time. That might have been the most excitement I'd had inside the house, since—ever!

Nicki was running around too . . . only I didn't believe her enthusiasm was as joyous as mine was. She was darting here and there, cradling her phone on the side of her neck, her hands flying in different directions as the pinhole leaks in the pipes created a waterfall. I watched her grab buckets and towels to catch and sop up the water, all the while pleading with me to stop slogging my soppy feet throughout the house. Well, I wanted to cooperate—but she'd have to catch me first! What a fun-filled afternoon.

Ironically, that was the beginning of the week when Nicki was researching the seventh law of karma, the law of focus. It's about knowing the best place to put your attention to get where you want to go, and keeping it there as much as you can. Not easy to do when the sky is falling into your kitchen!

Being a canine companion to a human, I know some things about focus. The place I put my attention most often is on Nicki, of course. But sometimes I do have to split my focus: dinnertime, Nicki; treat time, Nicki; the pets and smiles of strangers, Nicki; walking with Jake and his human . . . Nicki. But through all those activities, even if I'm distracted for a second, I can keep at least one eye on my favorite prize.

It seems much harder for humans to remain focused on what they really want and need, especially when things get a little chaotic. Today, wall after wall has been stripped open, showers and toilets are being moved, baseboards are being replaced, and new drywall is going in all around. This particular transformation will likely take many months before it's all done. But when it is, the house will be right as rain again. And Nicki will have an easier time focusing on . . . focus!

It all reminds me of the time I tried to lick an ice-cube tray fresh out of the freezer, and my nose got stuck to it. I learned how to fly that day as I tore around the room in a panic. I can assure you: that focused my attention—on getting unstuck!

I know this isn't the first time Nicki has had an awful lot to handle and had a hard time knowing the right thing to do next. There have been times when she's had to manage a lot of things all at once that are no fun, and all by herself, without me. But I think that might be one reason why she's so good at figuring out how to clean up a messy situation. I think it comes down to this: *you focus your attention on where you want to be after all the dust settles, and let that image guide you through.*

Marrying Mike

Sandra entered the dress shop the same way her brother, Mike, regularly entered a room: with a big grin and a loud voice, stealing the show every time. I think growing up in their family might have included competition between the two of them, specifically for who could roll out the best punch line first.

"As your maid of honor, I insist that you announce what color and style you're choosing. I'm flexible, but I refuse to wear anything that doesn't highlight my boobs," she said.

"Okay," I laughed. "So what do you think about peach? I think my mum would love it."

"Are you serious? That's the one color I can't wear! It makes my skin look washed out. Pleassse, any color but peach!" she pleaded.

"No worries. Choose the color you like then," I conceded. It seemed more important to her than to me.

Sandra tried on a light-blue summer dress

with a deep, plunging neckline and a knee-length skirt.

"This is it!" she declared, moving her feet in an attempted cha-cha, while her outfit and exaggerated cleavage swished from side to side.

I started to realize that I honestly didn't care what people wore to my wedding. Things were moving so fast, and I was in an unfamiliar town, at the mercy of everyone else. I was feeling unmoored.

My wedding "gown" was a long chiffon summer dress with spaghetti straps and no frills. It was just a simple white dress, and under a hundred dollars, which appealed to my English upbringing not to be wasteful. How could I go wrong with that?

"Are you sure that's what you want?" Sandra asked, questioning my sense of occasion.

"It's exactly what I want," I replied as I headed back into the dressing room.

"When are your parents coming in? Have they arranged their flights yet?" she asked through the door.

"Yes, they'll be flying in to Toronto," I said, thinking for a moment about my own Canadian experience. "They're staying in Niagara Falls for the night, then making their way here."

I looked at the dress again in the mirror. I'd never had an occasion to wear something this long before. A wave of nervousness came over me—was it normal to have cold feet? The reality was sinking in. I was getting married!

. . .

Things came together in a whirlwind, and my parents arrived the day before the wedding. But the next morning, Mike and his friends were somewhat out of hand; they were still "celebrating" from the night before.

"Did you see that guy in the penguin suit, Daryl? Oh, hang on—it's just me in the mirror! Whoa, I look good, right? I hope no one mistakes me for double-oh-seven or something. Things could turn ugly pretty fast if that happened!"

Mike roared at his own jokes while Daryl and the other guys dropped to the ground and rolled around like it was the funniest thing they had ever heard.

Years later, Mike told me that he and his friends had been doing LSD, which explained how, in an instant, Mike's euphoric state swung from silly to serious to paranoid. It was definitely not a memorable, Hallmark kind of day, but I did enjoy spending time with my mum and dad. And with Sandra's jokes, I was able to keep smiling.

Honeymoon on Seneca Lake

The word "honeymoon" is derived from the Old English term *hony moone*. The "hony" part refers to both the sweetness of a new marriage and the European custom of giving newlyweds mead—alcoholic liquor made by fermenting honey and water—on their wedding day. The "moon" part refers to the time it takes for the moon to go from full to waning to full again; that is, one month. So, the couple would be given a month's worth of mead in hopes that the sweetness of the marriage would last that long. That's right, just a single month.

You could say that Mike took this definition to new levels.

We'd decided to rent a houseboat for a week on Seneca Lake, one of the largest of the glacial Finger Lakes in New York State, and the deepest of them. On our first night, I woke up to the rocking of the houseboat. We were drifting far from shore, the wind had picked up, and I panicked when I realized that Mike had *already* consumed enough alcohol to last a month. He had passed out before setting the anchor. I had hoped for a more romantic evening together; it was our honeymoon, after all. I thought love would be in the air, but sadly, it wasn't.

I tried to wake up Mike. He became conscious only long enough to complain that I had awoken him.

"Shut up," he snapped. "Everything's fine."

But everything wasn't fine. The anchor wasn't engaged. He had thrown it overboard, but never set it. We weren't supposed to be moving, and we were. I didn't know what to do. I lay awake that night, sober and scared, listening to the wind move across the water and the waves break against the sides of the boat. In my hours of fear, I knew I should never again leave my safety, my fate, in someone else's hands. But I had put myself in this situation, and now I would have to make the best of it.

When the sun came up, Mike didn't seem to remember snarling at me—and I didn't want to remember it either. He quickly used humor to change the mood, and I went with it. But I insisted we dock the boat on shore for the rest of the week. I told him that I'd been feeling seasick on the open water, and it would be calmer close to land.

Being on shore didn't change Mike's behavior. As soon as we moored at the marina, he started drinking again, and when the sun went down, it was blackout time once again. He drank all day for every day of our honeymoon. I didn't try to track how much; it didn't matter. By the second day I knew that once the fun and charm wore off, the inebriated resentment would always kick in. Our marriage was in trouble before it even started. There was no anchor set to keep it stable.

It was the start of a spiral of darkness. I had no feelings of safety or intimacy. I often wonder how nice it would be to go back to that younger self, pick her up, and save her from the world she was walking into. It was the world that Mike's own mother had warned me about.

Going Back to Marco

As we packed up the car for our long drive back to Florida, I stood firm. My total focus was on Marco Island. I wasn't going to stay in Buffalo. By now it was cold—this was November 1984—and I knew the weather would remind me of England and the winters I had left for good. And anyway, the yacht club where Mike was bartending had closed for the season.

Dot tried hard to convince Mike and me to stay with her.

"You wouldn't need to wait tables. You could stay home and take care of me," she said. "Mike can go back to work at the club after the winter."

I thought a lot of Dot, but I knew I didn't want her life. I would be happy to wait tables if it took me back to the island I loved.

"Maybe we should stay," Mike said as I closed the trunk.

"Are you really going down that road again?" I said in disbelief. "We're going. The deposit is down on our apartment, and if we're going to have a normal marriage, we need to make this change. My mind is made up."

My determination was really about more than the weather. Moving back to Marco seemed our last hope for a relationship that looked anything like a marriage, which Mike and I had not yet consummated—a fact Mike pinned on living at his mother's house. The honeymoon had been little more than a one-man drinking party. By this point, I had started to question whether there was something wrong with me. I didn't yet understand Mike's condition—that excessive alcohol and drug abuse can cause impotence. I didn't yet understand that, potentially, our relationship could never be normal. Whenever I asked him about it, he told me that things would be better when we got our own place. I was only twenty-three, and I believed him.

Mike's friends and family said good-bye, fully expecting us to return in the summer, as Mike did every year. But there was one thing I knew for sure: I had no plans of ever coming back.

. . .

I felt reenergized being on Marco Island again, with the warm ocean breezes and calm, friendly people. Work was plentiful, and I found a job at the north end of the island in a quaint little restaurant with a menu full of fresh seafood. I served Shrimp Lenny and Snapper De Marco to my regular customers, who always showed their appreciation. I was happy to see them, and it felt good to be back in paradise.

Mike, on the other hand, only became angrier and more distant with time. On one particular afternoon he came to see me at the restaurant after what was clearly an early start to his drinking. I had arrived before my shift to find a quiet space at one of the corner tables, excited about a new career idea—I had started a course to get my real estate license. I was preparing for the exam, and the restaurant was a perfect setup. I would study during the day and then work hard at night to rake in the tips.

But to Mike, my ambitions amounted to nothing more than another opportunity for a put-down.

"Those books are worthless, as worthless as you. What a waste of time and money. What do you need a career for? You could have stayed up north and you wouldn't have had to work at all."

"You married the wrong woman if you want to live in Buffalo," I told him. "You don't have to support my ideas, Mike, but don't try to crush them. You can choose to bartend, but I'm choosing a career in real estate."

"What the fuck is wrong with bartending for a living? My job isn't prestigious enough for you?"

"That's not at all what I meant," I said, looking around the restaurant. Some of the other servers were beginning to arrive. "Let's discuss this another time."

I hoped he'd get the hint that this wasn't the

time or place to continue this never-ending fight. It was a nice try at least.

"What you're doing is pointless. You'll never pull this off anyway. You're just wasting money!" he scolded before storming out. I quickly looked around to see if we had made too big a scene; I liked my job and surely didn't want to lose it like this. Thankfully, my coworkers were in the kitchen getting things ready for the evening rush, and my boss hadn't arrived yet.

It was astounding how quickly Mike's attitude toward me had changed once I said, "I do." That, plus his drinking—which seemed to be escalating, if anything—made me more homesick than I was willing to admit. I put aside those real estate books and focused on working more shifts, all the while keeping the details of my life hidden from the people around me. Months of this public deception turned into years, but I just couldn't let anyone know I had made such a huge mistake. I had taken a vow, and now I was left to honor it with my English stiff upper lip. Where I came from, you kept a lid on things like this.

Mike, however, only fell deeper into trouble. Drugs were coming into Marco Island regularly back then, and it was easy for a boat to make a drop-off from Miami. Regulations on the water didn't exist, and everyone working in the restaurants knew of someone caught up in the frenzied cocaine merry-go-round. "White powder people" surrounded Mike, and being a person with destructive, addictive behaviors, he was magnetically attracted to them.

I was so naïve concerning drugs that one time I cleaned the fridge and threw away what looked like a bag of baking powder. When Mike later discovered I'd thrown out his cocaine stash, he punched his fist through the car windshield—while I was driving! I watched the glass shatter before my eyes. The wall in our apartment was the next casualty of Mike's increasing anger. He punched through that too, leaving me to scurry about and patch up the damage. The next day as he nursed his swollen hand, he swore to me that it would never happen again. But of course, it always did.

I finally began to understand why Dot had warned me about what she saw happening with Mike. I had seen how damaged she was. I didn't have the miles of experience with this kind of life that she had, but I could already feel my stamina draining. The strength I had brought with me from England was drifting away. It was time to take those licensing exams and focus on getting that strength back.

Reshaping a Life

On April 1, 1987, I walked into a real estate office to start a new job and saw Doug for the first time. As I moved toward my desk, he stood up and smiled. I wanted so much to stop and talk with him and to learn from some of his experiences in a business that was so new to me. But I didn't want to draw attention to myself; I wasn't there to make friends, so I smiled and walked by. Doug sat back down. I kept to myself as my new career began. I needed to be successful here. I needed to pay some bills.

Unfortunately, my very first sale fell apart. My customer had been planning to use his grandchildren's college fund to purchase a waterfront lot, but he was nervous about it—so nervous that the next day he came by the office to terminate the contract. I had spent the time to find the perfect location for him, at an amazing price. Now he was sorry, he said, and I was too.

Thankfully, my next three deals happened quickly, but not without a glitch. I had switched floor duty with an agent named Millie who was unable to show up for her scheduled time slot. New agents were always being asked to cover the weekend shifts, so I often did. I was working on a Sunday when the phone rang. It was Gina, a lovely lady interested in Marco Island water-front property. Gina owned a restaurant in New Jersey, and we connected right away. At the end of the day, Gina decided not to fly to Marco to look at listings but to instead go ahead with purchasing via phone and fax. I found what she was looking for, and she was grateful and very happy. As was I! Finding her the right properties, sight unseen, was a tall order, but she signed all the contracts without even visiting the island. I felt honored to have her trust.

When Millie returned to work, she had a cow!

"That was my floor duty, my customer!" she screamed.

Initially I offered to share one of the com-missions to appease her. I was new at this and wanted to keep the peace. But more than that, it felt normal to try to make others *feel* better. As usual, my attempts weren't enough. Millie's husband weighed in, and they wanted all three commissions. It was the beginning of my real estate career, and already I didn't feel comfortable about the environment at the office.

The same thing was happening at home. Since the beginning, I had believed I could somehow help Mike feel better. I thought that if he couldn't get better, I must be partly to blame. I was in a marriage, after all; wasn't I supposed to make it work? Fed up with what everyone else wanted and felt entitled to take from me, I finally confronted Millie, telling her I would split one commission with her—but this would be the last time. Now it was time to confront Mike.

"I checked into our insurance policy today, and sure enough, it covers a six-week treatment program. I already made the call for you, Mike," I announced.

"My drinking's not a problem. I can handle myself," he said, repeating his regular refrain. But this time I was persistent. This time I wouldn't give in.

"You cannot do it alone. You need help—they want to talk to you," I said.

I was sure that Mike's problems stemmed from the toxic environment of his childhood, created by his own alcoholic father. To Mike, perhaps his behavior felt *normal*. Yet I had to believe there was a way he could conquer the demons of his past; I was so sick of waging the uphill battle by myself. Finally, after much arguing and a threat to leave him, he agreed to get treatment. He got in a cab—entirely intoxicated. I stood and watched, helpless, as it drove away.

. . .

As the weeks of the program went by, I absorbed the valuable information provided to me at group meetings for spouses and families. I began to understand that, often, those caught up on either side of this cycle of destruction—either the alcoholic or the partner in the line of fire—have generations of addiction and abuse to overcome. I didn't have that hurdle and was curious how I had gotten caught up in this in the first place. I suppose rules don't apply when it comes to how powerful addiction can be, and how easily it can be overlooked in society. Swept under the carpet by anyone it touches, regardless of stereotypes, socioeconomics, or culture.

I knew it would be difficult for Mike to achieve permanent sobriety without professional help, and it would be critical that he change careers once the program was over. Abstention when surrounded by drinkers was not an option.

And, I learned, alcoholics in withdrawal are

prone to seizures and hallucinations, which was why a treatment program was so important in achieving a full recovery. But despite being in a program and even under the best of conditions, it doesn't work for everyone. Unfortunately, that was the direction things were going for Mike.

He seemed to do well at first; at least that's what he let everyone think. He would leave to attend all the meetings with a smile on his face and talk of the new lease on life he had been given. Everyone was proud of his efforts. I focused on fixing the home front, purchasing a new stereo system as if it were a prize, some kind of trophy for his efforts. I had high hopes he had turned his life around. Within a couple of months of his return home from treatment, however, the game was up. He admitted he hadn't actually been going to the meetings at all. We were right back where we had begun.

I was desperate. I had seen several other people in the program do very well, but I think Mike was unwilling to address his underlying emotional issues. And he was exceptionally skilled at flying under the radar to maintain his comfortable yet destructive lifestyle.

Mike's addictions turned him into a master

con artist who was just buying time. He knew how to maximize every situation to its full advantage, and now had prescription pills to add to his list of dependencies—using our joint bank account to finance his fixes. I was drained financially, emotionally, and spiritually. Something had to change.

. . .

Living in Florida—where the sun shined in December—the only time I missed cold weather was when Christmas rolled around, bringing with it memories of joyful times in England with family. But this year I once again found myself attending the office Christmas party alone. Meghan was in charge of the secret Santa program, an office-party ritual where everyone got to pick a name out of a hat. The idea was to wrap a ten-dollar gift for that coworker and bring it to the party.

"Which name did you pick?" Meghan asked. She could tell by my face that it was Millie!

Suddenly, I blurted out an idea that was much better than secret Santa. "How about taking the money for our gifts this year and donating everything to a family going through some hard times?"

Meghan laughed. "You can pick another name. I won't tell!"

"Seriously," I said. "I've been thinking about this all week. I want to give our secret Santa money to a child who hasn't had the greatest year. I want to give them a special Christmas."

"I'm on board," Meghan replied.

And there, amid the confusion of a distressing marriage, the Joy of Giving program for children who are down on their luck at Christmas time was born. I still run it to this day.

That was the beginning of the change I was looking for. Pining away for my remembered Christmases back home wasn't getting me anywhere. I had to acknowledge my life as it was, and if I wanted to see change, I had to start with me. It was time to create something completely different—and 100 percent positive—in my life. Giving in this way lifted me up in those difficult years, and even today I am amazed that something so bright came from such a dark time. Today, the Joy of Giving reaches hundreds of children every year.

. . .

It was the day after Christmas, Boxing Day 1990. "This shit is cold!" Mike yelled as he threw his plate. Gravy and cranberry sauce splattered the walls. Lights from the artificial tree illuminated the corner of the room as I fell to my knees and looked at the mess around me. I had no words or energy to respond to Mike. Instead, I found myself just staring at the twinkling lights on the branches. Bored by my lack of reaction, Mike stumbled into bed for the night. All the while, I continued to stare at the tree. I began to think of the girl I had been before all this had happened. The zest I'd had to make my dreams come true. What had become of that determination and the visions of a life full of potential?

I began to pick up the broken pieces of the plate, and it struck me: for all the seven years we had spent together, my emotional focal point had been Mike. I had been waiting and hoping that he would somehow get better so our marriage would improve. But now, in this moment, in the clarity of the Christmas lights before me, I finally grasped that looking to him for the change I needed would not work. The only person who could heal Mike was Mike, and the only person in this world I had the power to heal was myself.

At this lowest of low points, I was overcome with the desire to go home. It had been years since I'd been back to England. I wanted to be rid of this constant hurt and of the person I had become. It was time to find my strength again and to make some tough decisions. I picked up the phone and booked a flight to London. I would leave in June when work was slow. I realized I had been living in denial for so long and it was time to focus on myself. Soon I would be able to get some physical distance from Mike, and he would no longer be the focus of my energy. *From this point on, I would lift my attention up and out of my broken marriage and aim it toward my own future.*

The Eighth Law of Karma: Giving

A Kind Heart Can Transform the World

Be kind

There's something beautiful here—the birds. And even though I've lived around them all my life, they sometimes do things that surprise me. Last night, for instance, I was outside when two ibises flew into the yard. Have you ever seen an ibis? They're white like me, but very tall and slender, and they have long skinny beaks. They're very dignified these birds, and when they see me or another dog coming close, they usually walk calmly away, head held high. They know they can fly away if they really have to.

But this time when I approached them, they stayed right where they were, just looking at me, then at each other, and then back at me. So I walked right up and sat down on the grass beside them. I was surprised they let me, and I looked back toward Nicki. She was smiling at us, watching two white birds and one white dog enjoy the fresh air together, nobody in a hurry, nobody skittish or antsy, just sharing a peaceful moment.

I think the ibises stayed beside me because I've absorbed Jake's calm wisdom, and it's now a part of me. Next time I see him, I will thank my friend for that moment with the beautiful white birds.

But Jake's been going through a tough patch lately. That spot on his nose has turned out to be a problem. His human family is trying all kinds of fancy new treatments, and we're all giving him lots of attention and affection as we walk this path with him.

Jake's not a pup anymore, and the therapies have slowed him down. So these days I take extra care to match his pace. I adjust myself to what Jake needs, and it's not so hard. After all, it was Jake who showed me the value of putting someone else front and center and doing whatever you can for them. He did that for me so many times when I was a younger pup. Through his example, I learned that there's nothing more important than love and kindness. Really, it's the only way to live.

And Then Came Cheena

In April of 1991, while I was at work one day, Mike's friend Carl came by our apartment to tell Mike that the shih tzu puppies he and his girlfriend had bred to make some extra money were almost old enough to find new homes.

During the previous night's drunken rage, Mike had returned to an old grievance: "It's all your fault that I don't have any children," he roared at me, his face red.

I responded more quietly but with equal fury. "I'd never bring children into this environment with you, even if you were capable of conceiving them! You're not fit to be a parent!"

Carl's visit had given Mike a new argument to start, which he tossed at me when I got home from work: if we didn't have children, we should at least have a dog. It made no sense to me—what did one have to do with the other? But I was sick of fighting, and bone tired, and I gave in. I had no illusions: I knew the responsibility for the dog would be entirely mine—Mike was barely able to take care of himself, much less a dog. But I told him, fine! I would stop by to see the puppies after work the next day.

Carl lived in a small new development on Marco Island. His condo was a bachelor pad with most of the living space contained in one room, so I saw the puppies as soon as I walked in.

I had done my best to be objective and rational before going over to check them out; in fact, I had carefully listed for myself all the reasons I shouldn't get a dog. But I knew that if I took the plunge, I would want a girl. There were two girls in the litter: one pure white and the other, a smaller puppy, black and white. I found myself instantly drawn to the smallest; as soon as I picked her up, I knew I never wanted to put her down again. For the first time in a long while, I felt something inside me that I had almost forgotten existed. I felt . . . love.

Although the puppies wouldn't be ready to leave their mum for another week, I asked Carl if I could bring her home for a few hours to see how she would take to me. It was just an excuse—I wasn't ready to part from her, but I had to be patient. The day I picked up my pup, I drove over to my friend Jean's to show her off. Jean was one of the kindest people on the planet. Today I can see how lucky I was to have had her as my role model for many years.

Jean and her husband, Bob, were members of the yacht club in Olcott where Mike worked—that's how I met them. They spent their summers on Lake Ontario and traveled south to Marco Island in the wintertime. Jean was a petite woman with bleach-blonde hair and fabulous taste in clothes. Despite the fact that she had money to burn, she was down to earth, and she always gave generously of her love to those around her, especially to dogs.

I sat on a stool at Jean's breakfast bar while she poured herself a scotch. Then she joined me in the living room, where she proceeded to get down on her hands and knees and take a good look at my two-pound pooch.

"Let's get a look at this little girl, shall we?" she said. "You need a name, you sweet thing." Jean looked intently at my puppy while scratching the fur around her ears. Then she ran through a few popular names. "Holly. Or Daisy."

"That's a good start," I replied tentatively, repeating them in my mind to see how they felt. Then, after a few more moments of contemplation,

Jean said, "You know, I'm thinking she looks a little like a panda. 'China' keeps popping into my mind for some reason. Maybe something like China?"

"Now we're getting somewhere!" I said. I liked the sound of it.

"China . . . China," she repeated. "I like that name."

"Or . . . Cheena. China, Cheena." I mumbled on.

"That's it, Che-e-e-ena. I love it!" Jean declared. "Cheena Ling."

And that was it, her name. I was hopelessly and completely in love.

. . .

By June, Cheena had become a grounding force in my life. Being with Mike for so many years had taken its toll, but at last I had something that brought happiness to my days. My goal lately had been to increase my clientele and focus on working to better my financial situation. I felt life evolving around me again, and I believe Cheena was the catalyst that made that happen. She did an excellent job of pulling me into a more positive mind-set.

I had never had a dog before, and I didn't realize how deep my attachment to her could be. She took away all the bad energy. Had I known the love I would feel for her, I might never have booked a flight, because now I had to leave Cheena behind for my planned trip to England, and my heart was torn. I considered canceling, but my ticket was paid for, and my family had made plans for various get-togethers. I couldn't disappoint them.

Plus, I longed to go back and see everyone again, and I needed to sort out what to do with the rest of my life because, sadly, not even Cheena could fix the mess of this marriage. I wanted to believe Mike's promise that he would be on his best behavior, but I still shortened my trip to a week.

I put Cheena's photo in my purse, and she watched me from the window as I drove away. I missed her already. But I was on my way to London. This time tomorrow, I'd be back in Bromley.

· · ·

Growing up in Bromley, my life had reflected two totally different worlds, differences I didn't distinguish at the time but rather loved as a normal way of life. My dad was one of seven kids, and there were lots of hand-me-down clothes in his childhood. My mum, on the other hand, had more privileges, such as holidays, hired cars, and chauffeurs. Her lineage was more refined than my dad's, but both sides of the family honored life with all of their hearts.

My first visit on this trip was to my dad's side of the family. For as long as I could remember, the most laughter-filled times were found at my cousin's pub, and that's where we all headed. Camaraderie over a pint in my cousin's company had always made me feel welcome, and tonight was to be a special family celebration.

When the fun was under way, everyone started singing. Someone made a toast to my aunt and uncle's ruby anniversary—their fortieth. I felt like no time had passed at all.

"Hello, Finn," I said to my cousin. I hadn't seen him for many years, but he looked the same as I remembered. He poured me a drink from behind the bar.

"Hello, Nic!" he said, as if he'd just seen me last week.

My relatives surrounded the microphone, and they could sure harmonize a well-formed tune with their incredible voices. I didn't inherit that gene! As the night progressed, songs turned into stories, many of which I'd heard before, like the one about my dad's older brother, the great boxer who, when he was a lad, received a trophy from the king of England. As always, I loved hearing stories from when my parents were young. It's difficult to imagine some of the hardships they went through during the war. When my dad was a boy, for instance, he and his siblings were split up and sent to live in the countryside of Somerset, away from the bombing of London. My dad went to live with a kind lady named Rose.

"Life was tough back in our day," Dad started. He looked toward his brother-in-law, Jim, the man he saw as a father figure and loved most in the world. As kids, we had often heard the stories he was about to launch into. He'd joke about the times he had to walk to school with holes in his shoes (this much was true), uphill both ways, during a snowstorm no less! On this night, however, his tone was softer. He wasn't joking; you could see the pain in his eyes as he began.

"I remember being in the classroom down in the countryside when old, dodgy Mrs. Dorsey came right up to my desk and informed me, in front of the whole bloody class, that my mum had died. Then she turned away with not so much as a hand of support, while I stood there fumbling for the handkerchief in my pocket." He paused for a moment to take a sip of beer. "I've never been able to erase that feeling since I was six years old," he sighed.

"Those were some tough days, all right," Uncle Jim confirmed, and pulled his pint to his lips.

My dad was such a strong and supportive person in my life: determined, passionate about life, and kindhearted. When I heard his story, I was instantly brought back to my own feelings about the Bromley schools and how disconnected the teachers seemed to be from their students—except for Mrs. Flowers, of course.

The evening conversations continued. Uncle Jim told the story of the day he taught Dad to drive, and everyone at the table started laughing so loud that I couldn't hear the end of the story. There was such a sense of fun and an outpouring of love throughout the night; it was all I could do to just soak it up as fast as it came my way. My family didn't know how broken I was inside. No one really knew Mike, so no one asked questions about him. Instead tales came up about Simon, and how he had married a Scottish girl who was "crazier than a barn owl." They had just one child, a son. I wondered what my life might have been like if he had come to meet me in America after all.

After visiting Dad's side of the family, it was time to enjoy some traditions of my mother's side. Mum's brother took us to Royal Ascot, a favorite event for our family. A highly anticipated thoroughbred horse race, Royal Ascot takes place each summer and is revered for socializing, fashion, and style. The race has been run for more than three hundred years, and it showcases some of the best racehorses in the world. Each year the event is broadcast to audiences around the globe, but experiencing it in person is something altogether more special. It is a spectacle of tradition, excitement, and color. I loved watching the royal procession as it passed by the elegant lawns to loud cheers from the crowd. Such an unforgettable atmosphere—champagne, food stalls, picnics on the lawn, and up-close views of the horses and riders as they headed out onto the track.

In anticipation of this special event, before I left Marco Island I had shopped for a hat to bring with me. I chose an extravagant, gold, glittery sailor cap that was ultra-American—so much so that my cousin thought there was a chance I might not be allowed into the event because I was wearing something so nontraditional.

"Seriously, Nic," he pleaded. "Where on earth did you find that hat? You do know that there are specific guidelines on what you can wear. It says somewhere that novelty clothing is not permitted on the site. Do you have a backup hat?"

"Well, Charlie, I guess this symbolizes my American transformation then. I like it. If they don't let me in, it will be their loss!" I joked.

To all my relatives' great relief, we had no trouble getting through the gates. Instead of being denied, I was actually televised that day. The commentators were highlighting the outfits and hats—of the proper elegant English variety— when the camera zoomed right in on me and the speaker made note of "one of the most vibrant and unique hats in the crowd."

"You can take the British girl out of America, but you can't take America out of the British girl," I laughed.

My visit home was everything I had hoped for, though I think I drove everyone a little bonkers with how often I flashed my picture of Cheena, as though she were my real live flesh and blood. I missed her like crazy, and showing her off helped me hide how badly things had turned out for my marriage.

I left my loving family in Bromley that week, along with a lot of the fear that had been holding me back. Going home to England didn't just fill me with courage again; it reawakened my spirit—the place in my core that had taken me to Marco Island in the first place. The company and attention of so many generous, kind, loving people had lifted me up. I could feel my passion again and clearly see how important it was that I take back control of my life. From that point on, I would make decisions that were right and healthy for me.

As I sat on the plane, I felt ready. A sense of resolve came over me while I reflected on the years leading up to this moment. I was grateful to be going back to America. It was time to face the truth.

. . .

I walked through the door to find Mike stretched out on the sofa with Cheena next to him. He moved, and she yelped. Instantly, I smelled something burning. I dropped my bags. *Oh no, it's Cheena's hair!* Embers from Mike's cigarette had fallen onto her fur while he lay there, oblivious. I ran straight over to pick her up and rushed her to the kitchen sink to run cool water over her back.

"Mike! What the hell?" I shouted, adrenaline coursing through me. I felt a strength that had been dormant for too long. "This is the last time I'll ever leave Cheena alone with you," I yelled. I was incensed and didn't care if he knew it.

Mike stirred out of his booze-induced slumber in defense mode. He didn't have a dinner plate handy to throw this time, so instead he reached for the fine bone china dish with the American Lady butterfly that I proudly displayed on the living room table. He pulled his arm back and, with all of the strength he could muster, pitched it in my direction.

"Bitch!" he growled.

Because he was lying down, it was a low throw heading straight for the mirrored wall opposite the sofa. I instinctively put my foot out to stop the plate. It hit my anklebone and did not break.

Coming back to Mike felt like a rerun of a bad movie. I was determined this would be the last scene. The curtain was down.

"I want a divorce," I said calmly.

My marriage was over.

Part 3—Love, Love, Love

Karma, when properly understood,
is just the mechanics through which
consciousness manifests.
—Deepak Chopra

The Ninth Law of Karma: Here and Now

All We Really Have Is This Moment

Be

Everywhere on Marco Island, the vegetation is lush, and our yard is wonderfully so. We have a grassy area with two beautiful royal palms, great big old things. In another spot is our grapefruit tree; humans like to drink the juice of those fruits, but blah! they're too bitter for me. All around are hibiscus plants, covered with large red flowers. Then there are the white gardenias— Nicki loves the fragrance, and sometimes I do too, but other times it's more than my canine nose can handle, and I have to go sniff around in the dirt.

In the evenings, we like to sit outside together and look off to the west toward the setting sun and watch its razzle-dazzle show. I'm happy to sit beside Nicki, and I love this time of day to stop for a belly rub. I guess after seven years on this planet as a dog you learn a thing or two about how to be! It's nature's way.

When Jake comes over, I have to slow down even more. Jake is tired a lot now, and though I know he's happy to visit us, he doesn't say much these days. I miss Jake's stories. But now that my old friend is quiet, and his beard is speckled with white, it's still nice to sit beside him and sniff the breezes together. And we're good at being in the moment; dogs are just like that, always alert to our surroundings and the people and places in our lives. Now Nicki? She's not always as good at it as she'd like to be. Humans have that problem sometimes, worrying about the future or fretting about the past. That's why one of my most important jobs is to keep my favorite person right here, right now. I am here to remind her that *the present moment is the best place to be.*

Freedom

I was thirty years old when I left the attorney's office with separation documents in hand. I didn't need paperwork to tell me my marriage was over, but now it was official. I could finally move on. It would take only three more months for the judge to sign the divorce decree.

Mike wasn't prepared to take on the mortgage by himself, so I had secured first and last months' rent for him on a one-bedroom apartment, and he was finally moving out. He refused to believe it was for good. I wanted the condo and I needed to stay put, as a rental wouldn't allow me to keep my dog. She was my life, so I had agreed to the debt if Mike agreed to leave Cheena with me. Mike got in his car, towing the boat, and drove away with what savings we'd had—it was all his now. I had taken the boat loan, car loans, and credit card loans.

My attorney thought I was nuts, of course. "This is a terrible deal for you," he told me. But I didn't care. If that was the price of getting that part of my life behind me, so be it. Now that I could see the finish line, I just wanted the divorce to be over, and fast. I needed a clean break from the old, unhealthy energy I had lived with for so long. I wanted peace—and freedom, and there was no price too dear for that. All I had truly cared about was that the paperwork stipulated that I got Cheena. And it did, on the very first page. Now it was time to rebuild my life. As I sat in front of the notary and witnesses, I took a deep breath. I put my pen to the paper, and it was done.

Jean became my coach as I navigated my new path. She always enjoyed life; it truly seemed like she didn't worry about the future or get hung up on the past. She loved company, and when you spent time with her, you spent a lot of it laughing—and eating; she always made sure you had enough to eat. She took me out to dinner everywhere on the island. At her favorite place, Jean usually ordered the lamb chops or anything she could take home for her dog. I always ordered Chicken Francese and saved half for Cheena.

"Cheers, Nic," Jean said the evening I signed the papers, raising her glass at the start of our meal. "To your new life—it's about time. To you!"

I went out searching for this new life, and

that started with dating. It was fun, and I loved the freedom. I found it impossible to trust any man, but that was okay because I wasn't ready to get serious with anybody—for years, my whole life had been nothing but serious! It was time to loosen up and lighten up. For a while I played the field, and I was perfectly happy to join in the power games and manipulation of the dating scene—at first. But soon enough, the more I tried to embrace my newfound power over men, the more separated from myself and my own truth I became. I still trusted no one except Jean, and despite all the male attention I was getting, I was starting to feel alone.

. . .

On December 11, 1992, it had been exactly a year since I'd called my parents and opened the conversation with two words: "I'm divorced." They'd had no idea how bad things were between Mike and me until that very moment. But after all the anger and sadness, in the end, declaring my independence had been as simple as that. I had put the dark years behind me and kept what was worth salvaging: Cheena and the annual Joy of Giving program, the lights of my life.

I had changed and was no longer that young English girl who came to the US for her shot at the American dream. I had grown and was an independent American woman now. I had worked hard and gotten myself out of debt and found myself less interested in the chaos of empty relationships and started letting them all go. I had enough love in my heart for myself, and after what I'd been through, I didn't expect anyone to give me what I knew I deserved. I was developing a sense of confidence and calm, just as I was, now on my own.

. . .

In July of 1993, I was hovering over the copy machine in the kitchen at my office when my colleague Doug walked by on his way to the coffee station. I knew that the annual two-day mini lobster season was to start the following week—a time when anyone can dive for lobster before the commercial season starts—and that Doug and his two teenagers went every year.

"Are you going to the Keys again this year?" I asked him.

"I sure am," he said. He topped off his cup with fresh coffee and then circled back to the copy machine, which was chugging along making duplicates of my latest sales contract. "We're staying in Key West. You dive, don't you? Why don't you join us?"

"Well, I'm certified . . . " I wasn't exactly confident about my diving skills, and I'd been caught off guard by the invitation.

"I'm bringing my kids," he said without hesitation. "Come with us—it'll be fun."

"I might take you up on that, if I can find someone to take care of my dog." It was the first thing that I blurted out of my mouth, and I wondered if he could tell how excited I felt at the thought of spending time with him in the Keys. I tried to stay cool as he reached out and handed me the copies. He was now standing so close I thought he might have been able to hear my heart pounding in my chest.

I had worked at the same real estate office with Doug for six years now. He was always kind, polite, respectful—everything Mike wasn't. I had liked him from the day I met him. I knew he had moved to Marco Island in 1985 after his parents, who lived on the island, had been in a devastating head-on car collision that resulted in his mother's death. He'd packed up his life in Indiana and moved here to care for his father. I also knew that Doug was quite the bachelor. He'd had a difficult divorce several years earlier and often declared that he'd never get married again. So far—despite receiving his share of proposals—he had succeeded in staying unattached.

Yes, I did want to join him in the Keys! But I wasn't an experienced diver. In fact, I'd only been on one dive trip before, and it was a disaster. It had come terrifyingly close to being my last act in this life.

The conditions had been dangerous to begin with, and as an inexperienced diver—it was my first time diving in the ocean—I had no frame of reference for just how poor they were. Our captain knew, though, and he warned us to stick close to the boat. But Mike, being Mike, ventured off instead. Because he was my buddy-system dive partner, I followed him, and suddenly we were drifting quickly away with the current as it swept us out to sea.

All at once I realized I could see no sign of the other divers from our group. I signaled to Mike to go to the surface. At first, he ignored me; the visibility worsened, and soon I could barely see him. I poked at him until he finally agreed to ascend, but by that time I couldn't see our boat—or any boat. Now I was terrified. Mike was blind to the danger that I could plainly see. He descended again and surfaced—with rumors of sharks, his lame idea of humor.

"It's so deep I can't reach the bottom, and there's lots of shark bait in this water," he informed me—a cruel and unnecessary comment. I looked down through my mask to see swarms of tiny silver fish circulating below us.

Now, disoriented, I was starting to panic. For all I knew, the ocean floor was a hundred feet below me, not the thirty feet I had signed up for. Where were the other divers? Where was the boat? That boat was my lifeline now—literally. As I bobbed on the water, grateful at least for the flippers and buoyancy device that kept me afloat, memories of our honeymoon flooded back. Once again we were adrift without an anchor, even though I had promised myself I would never let that happen again.

Mike descended again, and now I was out in the ocean alone.

The captain of our excursion was seconds away from calling the Coast Guard to start searching for us when one of the divers on board the boat caught sight of something reflecting far in the distant sunlight—my fluorescent pink snorkel. I was saved! As the diving party made its way toward us, I waved my arms frantically.

With the sensory memory of that nightmare in my body, the more I thought about meeting Doug in the Keys, the more unsure I became. On top of that, my car had just come out of the shop but was still in need of repair. Jean was traveling in Upstate New York at the time and happened to call. When she found out I was considering driving my still-broken car to meet Doug, she put her foot down. She didn't want me to take the chance that it might break down again along the way and leave me stranded.

"We'll need to find a different way for you to get to the Keys for your weekend with Doug," she said. "Nic, this could be fun. Go!"

"I've been a bit worked up over the whole diving thing really," I told her. "Perhaps I should call Doug and cancel."

"Call it off? No way. I think your car breaking down is just a sign that you need to travel in style. You'll take my new baby."

"Your new convertible?" I cried. "That's crazy! No one has even driven it yet." The car had been delivered to her house, ready for Jean's return to the island in the fall.

"You deserve to go," she declared. "I won't take no for an answer."

"But—"

"Take the car."

I accepted Jean's offer, and the next day I was off to Key West in a brand new convertible with the top down, grinning from ear to ear.

. . .

When I arrived, Doug was already there with his kids and their friends. I unloaded my gear, and bumped into Doug in the elevator. He seemed glad to see me.

"You made it! Great timing. I ordered lunch for all of us, so as soon as I pick it up, we can go." I could see right away how much he was enjoying his time in the Keys. He looked so tanned and relaxed.

"I'll go," I offered. I was practically bursting with nervous energy and eager for something to do.

"Well, that would be great," Doug said. "I'll gas up and load the gear." At the café next to the hotel, I walked into the sounds of reggae. A guy playing the steel drums asked me, "Hey, món, how's the day?"

The atmosphere was relaxed and friendly and I went with it. "Well, actually, I'm about to go on my first date with a guy and his kids. A scuba diving date, no less. I'm going out on the water with a group of practiced divers who think *I* can dive too!"

"Live and let live, lady," he replied. And then he started to sing, his voice merging with the drums. "*Could you be loved . . .*"

I took his advice, and lunch, with me because once on board, I was faced with another rookie problem. I needed a dive platform. Doug seemed to sense my confusion. "Have you ever dived off a boat this size before?"

"Actually, no. How in the world do you get in the water?"

"It's easy, really. You just sit on the edge with your back to the water, and then do a backflip."

Yeah, right, I thought, sure I was going to embarrass myself. I watched his kids do exactly what he had described and it turned out to be easy! I backflipped in and surfaced laughing, relieved that at least that was over, and then I waited for Doug. We descended together until we stood on the bottom. He took my hand, and off we went to find lobsters. I still had no idea how to do that, but I didn't care. I felt safe. And I wanted him to hold my hand forever—to never let go.

The current in the shallow waters was mild,

and it was peaceful down there. We were surrounded by dozens of multicolored fish. One in particular caught my eye, a parrot fish, its tiny fins flapping with excitement, and I could have sworn he was smiling. Armed with what's called a tickle stick and a net, we started catching lobsters right away, prodding them out from beneath ledges and out of crevices. Sometimes it was challenging to get at them, and you had to work pretty hard at it, but it was still the most fun I'd had in so very long.

By the time the day came to a close, all my fears about diving had vanished. Doug cooked us the freshest lobster I had ever tasted in my life. It had been a lot of work physically, and it was certainly a long way to travel for a lobster dinner, but it was unforgettable, well worth investing the time and living with all my doubts and fluttery nerves leading up to the day. I was surprised to notice my guard coming down.

On our last night there, Doug and I headed to Mallory Square as the sun splashed its final wisps of vibrant orange and pink across the sky. There was an outdoor street party with magicians, jugglers, and even performing cats. We strolled down Duval Street, hitting every bar, like a pub crawl on the old Kent Road of London. At the end of the evening, I sat with an umbrella-festooned tropical drink in my hand. Doug reached out for my other hand. In that moment, my past felt a million miles away.

"Another round before we call it a night?" I asked Doug as I looked into his brown eyes.

He squeezed my hand a little tighter. "I don't need a drink," he said. "I have everything I need, right here—*right now.*"

The Tenth Law of Karma: Change

Your Life Lessons Repeat . . .
Until You Change Course

Trust in it

Lately I've been noticing how different each day is from the last, even when it seems like you're doing the exact same thing in the exact same place. Just yesterday the ocean was choppy and churning, but today it's tranquil: still, and smooth as glass. Sometimes, when the wind and the waves favor it, it's best to head out in the boat to Goodland. But on a calm summer day like this one, we change direction toward Keewaydin Island. It's a popular spot nearby where people like to take their dogs to run along the water's edge.

I look up into the endless sky and then down into the depths of the water below. Imagine being able to fly in the air or glide through the water. How exhilarating! I squint my eyes against the sun's reflection bouncing off the waves and sniff the wind. So many smells wafting toward us on the breeze, never in the same mix. Sometimes the deep, earthy smell of seaweed is the strongest, and other times it's the sharp tang of salt in the air.

After a few minutes, we slow down long enough to take in the perfection of it all. "We're close to the dolphin spot, Karma," Nicki says to me. She knows how excited I'll be about that. They're not always here, but today we're in luck. Three of them crest the water like synchronized swimmers, disappearing below the front of our boat where I'm sitting. I can barely contain myself. I bark out loud, "Come back!"

The smallest of the dolphins slows down and turns toward us. He swims slightly onto his side, exposing his smooth, gray, rubbery skin, one eye looking straight at me from above the waterline. I can tell he is as curious about me as I am about him.

It's all I can do not to jump into the water and swim with him. I know he'll be there to catch me. But I also know my humans would be upset if I dove overboard, so I sit tight and just enjoy the moment from where I am.

My new dolphin friend turns and dives beneath the boat again, but not before his tail fin smacks the surface hard, splashing salty water onto the deck and completely soaking me. Hey, that was fun! I shake off the water, knowing I'm in for a warm bath and blow-dry tonight.

We cruise through the emerald waters and on toward the white sand of Keewaydin Island. Everyone's here! There's Lulu and Salty, the friendly pair of rescues. Pepper, the proud Yorkie and Dreamer, the field spaniel, who lets his hair down once in a while and loves to run donuts in the grass with me. And Obi, the English terrier hanging from his human's arm. And then there's Grits, the white English Labrador who runs behind his human's golf cart each morning racing with Lucy. And stretched out on the sand is Meatball the Mastiff, who's the most docile, sweet tempered, pudgy thing you could ever meet.

Then I spot Jake. He's sitting in the shade of a low palm tree and watching all the fun. Jake's been changing, I notice. But then, we all have—we always do, don't we? We change like the shifting scents on the breeze on this beautiful day. Like the ripples of wind on water.

Leaving the Keys

All too soon, our weekend in the Keys was over. During those few days, time had seemed to stretch out forever, an endless stream of moments that touched my heart. But now we couldn't avoid returning to "real life" with all its schedules and tasks. We headed out for the trip home in a three-vehicle caravan: Doug's son towing the boat in front, Doug and his daughter in his Mustang convertible behind him, and me following everyone in Jean's car. Back at the dock, Doug had invited me to ride with him while his daughter drove Jean's car, but of course we couldn't do that—the car wasn't mine, after all.

We gassed up early, just after sunrise, knowing we could be bumper to bumper on the beautiful but narrow road, flanked by water on both sides, that was the only land route into or out of the Keys. When we pulled into the gas station, before I had a chance to grab my wallet out of the backseat, Doug picked up the pump's nozzle and started filling my tank.

No one had ever done that for me before. It was a small thing, but I could feel the care behind that simple gesture.

He walked up to my window and whispered, "Are you okay?"

"Never better," I smiled back.

Once we were back on the road, and I was alone with my thoughts, I realized how healing it had been for me to spend time with Doug. When I was with him, everyone and everything that had brought me pain seemed small and far away. He wanted to take care of me; that was so clear. And here I was, someone who had always shouldered responsibility for myself—not to mention for many other people in my life—experiencing that kind of generosity for the first time.

I smiled at the weekend's memories and then shook my head. I took a deep breath, looking for that heavy sense of needing to do more, to be more, that had always seemed to be there. I couldn't find it anywhere. I felt wholly at peace.

At that realization, I laughed out loud. I turned on the radio. And I sang along with it at the top of my voice for the rest of the long drive back to Marco Island.

A New World

I'd never dated anyone like Doug. His honesty was rare, and I knew I could trust him on every level. As I continued to see him, every day was a new experience for me. We went fishing and brought our catch of the day to restaurants to be prepared for us. He taught me how to play tennis, which was quite different than the squash I was used to from my days in England, and of course he let me win our match.

On the evening of my thirty-second birthday, Doug picked me up at my condo. I had already spent the day carrying out one of his lavish plans for me—relaxing in the sun at an invitation-only oceanside pool.

"How has your day been so far?" he asked, standing in the doorway, looking handsome and confident.

"Fan-tastic!" I beamed. "What have you got up your sleeve for tonight?"

"Well . . . I've made reservations at your favorite restaurant."

"Seriously? Do you even *like* Indian food?" I asked.

"I guess we're about to find out," he said.

We approached the restaurant, and the spicy aromas of Indian cuisine washed over us as we entered. Indian food always made me think of good times in England. Tonight I carried those memories with me while enjoying my new American paradise. It felt like the perfect blend of the different parts of who I was. Somehow Doug not only knew this—he nurtured it.

After dinner it was time to go to Doug's house to check on his dad, whose health was ailing—Doug cared for him morning, noon, and night. We pulled into the driveway and parked. Inside, Doug took a bottle of wine out of the fridge, and we headed for the lanai.

Cricket frogs hummed in the trees as we shared stories of our childhood days. We laughed a lot and we learned more about each other and about life that night.

Stepping Back

Three months had passed and things were going so well, almost too well somehow, if that were possible. I trusted Doug completely, but suddenly I didn't trust us. I had worked so hard for my independence. Was I ready to share my life with someone else again? What would happen to me if I got in deeper? And what made me think this—or any—relationship would, or even could, work out when I'd taken such a terrible wrong turn earlier in my life? Had I grown enough to do it better this time? I shook my head when I thought back to my divorce and the years of suffering that had led to it. Storm clouds were starting to blow in over my new paradise. I had to face what I was feeling: I was scared to let go any further into this relationship.

Rather than hiding it—how could I hide something like that from one of the most honest people I'd ever met?—I decided to explain to Doug what I was feeling. I would tell him that I was getting nervous and why. I didn't know how he'd take it, and that just made me even more anxious.

He listened with calm understanding, and then said, "Nic, it was your independence that I was first attracted to." From there he went on to say he just wanted to spend time with me—no more pressure than that. And then . . . he planned another great weekend for us, this time to see my first pro-American football game at what was then Joe Robbie Stadium. The game would be on December 19, 1993. Three days before the game, he gave me a sweatshirt as a gift, with a note: "I don't want you to be cold at the game. Love You! —D"

It was another small gesture, but so kind of him, and a sign of his constancy. He was clear about our relationship even as I wavered. He was comfortable trusting his inner voice. And as the days rolled by, and I spent more time in his calm presence, I began to trust mine too.

Fire!

Within six months, my cold feet were just a memory. We were a perfect example of how opposites attract and bring the best out in each other, and I was amazed with Doug's commitment to caring for his father, Fred.

Fred was born in 1909 and, at the age of eighty-four, still functioned well for the most part. His favorite pastime was watching baseball and cheering on his team to the end. "Looks like I won't see the Cubs win the World Series in my lifetime after all," he once told me. "But you watch—it will happen in yours."

Doug made sure his dad got good meals and took his medications. He also drove Fred everywhere he needed to go. Doug spent as much time with me as he could, but he checked in on Fred often, and he never left him on his own overnight.

But then one evening, after a late dinner at my place and a long day at work, unintentionally, we both fell asleep. I woke with a start when the phone rang around midnight. It was my neighbor Steph.

"Where's Doug?" she asked hurriedly.

"Mmmm . . . he's here with me, Steph," I mumbled. "Why? What's going on?"

"Doug's car is on fire out in front of your condo!"

"What are you talking about? How could Doug's car be on fire—?"

"I'm telling you, there's smoke coming out from the hood. It's on fire! I called the fire department before I called you. I hear the sirens. Is there anything important inside it?"

Doug dashed outside. I hung up the phone and followed him to the car, which was actually Fred's. Doug had flung the passenger's side door open and was retrieving papers from the glove box. He leaned in farther and grabbed some other belongings, then turned and headed back to the condo. Fire engines approached as the car became fully engulfed in black smoke.

As we watched the last of the flames being doused, I had a frightening thought. If Doug hadn't taken Fred's car tonight, it would have been parked inside his garage—and the results could have been devastating.

After the commotion with the fire department and police was sorted out, I drove Doug home to check on Fred. He was still awake and sitting in his favorite chair.

"It's late. Where have you been?" he asked Doug.

"Had a little electrical fire—problem with the car. Everything's okay now, though," Doug answered. He explained only a little more, keeping the details short to minimize Fred's concern.

Fred thought for a moment, with half a smile on his face. He looked at us, back and forth from one to the other, and then said, "Why doesn't your girl live with us, Doug? Then you wouldn't have to leave so much."

Doug turned to me. "Coming from Fred, that's a real compliment, and a good idea! Why don't you and Cheena move in?"

· · ·

Within a few weeks, I'd made arrangements to rent my condo and had started packing my things. Most of the work that needed doing was at Doug's place, however. He hadn't had much time for cleaning in the previous years; it had never been a priority before now. But after a great deal of elbow grease and after fifty bags of unwanted clutter were moved out, we found some space for me. I'd never seen the place looking better, and it wasn't long before I got to decorate for Christmas and put up our artificial tree, a shiny one.

Strands of clear lights lit it from top to bottom, while silver and gold decorations filled out its branches.

"How do you like the angel on the top?" I asked Fred.

"That could be you up there, girl," he said.

That settled it. This was home.

Vegas

It's funny: I can't remember exactly who asked whom to get married. Truly, we just stumbled into it. It might have begun with Doug talking about his first trip to Las Vegas with his dad, back in the day.

"I could walk into Castaways with two bucks and come out with twenty-eight," Doug told me, clearly pleased by the memory. He looked at Fred and laughed. "Remember I asked you that day, 'How long have you been holding on to this secret of making easy money?'"

Fred just grinned, the kind of smile that says there's more to the story than meets the eye. "It sure was exciting, with all the colorful lights, people crowded around the game tables, slot machines paying off."

"I'd love to take you there, Nic," Doug said. "The strip is solid neon lights and open twenty-four hours. Back then, when Fred and I used to go, there were weddings going on everywhere too, at all hours of the day and night. You could even get married at a drive-through."

"Seriously?" I asked. "Without getting out of your car?"

"Pretty sure you can still do that today," Doug said.

That must have been when it happened. The wheels started turning. I needed to see this city of lights. The idea of getting married in Las Vegas grew on both of us, and I found myself calling hotels to learn more.

It didn't take long to gather the details, and you didn't need a drive-through to make it easy to wed in Vegas. All you needed to do was pick a package—silver, gold, or platinum. The hotel would do the rest. It was effortless. The gold package, which included flowers, music, and photography, was perfect for us. We booked a one-week vacation in Vegas, the amount of time we could arrange for someone to take care of Cheena and Fred, and planned our wedding—no hassles and no stress. All we needed now were two witnesses.

I had stayed in touch with Arlene for a while after her move back to California from England, but it had been years since we last heard from each other, and she had been married and divorced. Then, unexpectedly, she had recently reached out to me, and when she learned what Doug and I were planning, she jumped at the chance to see me, and arranged to meet us at the Mirage, the hotel where we would be getting married. She agreed to bring a friend along. We had our witnesses.

When we got to Vegas, Doug and I spent a couple of days on our own. Then Arlene arrived and found us having lunch by the pool. I saw her walking toward us, dressed in her beautiful California style, tanned and fit as always. I jumped up with excitement.

I was thrilled to see her and gave her an enormous hug; happy tears welled up in my eyes.

"Where's your friend?" I inquired. "Did you come here with Mister Right?"

"Oh, he's parking the car. And no, he's another one to bite the dust," she sighed.

We started chatting as though no time had passed at all, catching up on the ins and outs of our failed relationships, including the one she had brought with her—a guy who was presently trying to chat up some girls at the pool. After she met Doug, she told me how happy she was for me. She definitely approved of my good taste. Then we reminisced about all the great food and conversations we'd shared back in England.

"I still love to cook, you know. It's one of my guilty pleasures in life," Arlene said. I gave her a look that said *and I still don't!* We exploded in laughter.

The wedding would be the next day. After dinner, I unpacked my dress and hung it in Arlene's room. I had done my best to keep Doug from seeing it despite bringing it on the plane in my hand luggage. When I'd shopped for it, I had actually planned something less extravagant, but I knew at first sight that this was my dress. When I had called my parents to let them know about my wedding plans, my dad had insisted on buying whatever dress I chose. I kept him to his word with that beautiful number.

. . .

It was a hot afternoon, a day to be grateful for air conditioning. While I got ready, I wore a gift Jean had given me the previous Christmas—a floor-length red-and-gold silk robe that looked like a Japanese kimono—even wearing it on the tram ride over to the beauty salon at Treasure Island. Once I was transformed into the bride-to-be, I met up with Arlene to get into my dress. Then we headed to the chapel to meet my man at the altar.

The door opened just as our song—Rod Stewart singing, "Have I Told You Lately That I Love You"—began to play. It was the tiniest of chapels, like landing on the other side of the rainbow in Munchkinland; I'd never seen an aisle so small. Tiny roses sat in tiny vases along the walls, and miniature garlands were draped above the altar. Beneath that stood the minister, who could have easily doubled as the wizard.

I loved it all—so much fun, and as easy as it gets. That's not to say that it didn't feel like a royal occasion. An amazing part of getting married in Las Vegas comes after the I-do's. You get to walk around all night in your wedding dress, and crowds part for you everywhere you go, clapping and cheering and smiling at you.

We got into a limo on the Strip and headed downtown to one of the original casinos. I was surprised to see a young girl out so late, standing next to her mum by the door. I noticed she had holes in her shoes. She looked up at me and then reached out with her dirty hands to touch my dress. Her mother hissed and slapped her hands away. "Off!"

"It's all good," I said. I knelt down, smiled at the girl, and gave her my bouquet of flowers—and hopefully a dream for a better future.

· · ·

Vegas amazed me—only in America could this be happening. A place built on the dream that it was "in the cards" to treat everyone, from all walks of life, as royalty. Toward the end of my week, I began to see more than just palaces: the decor and the rich red velvet reminded me of Nan and the sports book casino—it's true!—of my granddad. And then I realized that my original magical kingdom had been Christmas at my grandparents—just as grand—and I watched this new symbol of love and light come full circle.

. . .

How many times since meeting Doug had I been asked to trust that feeling of safety, to let go of painful memories and welcome the change that had come my way? How many times had Doug reinforced his trustworthiness with me, through actions large and small? Again and again, I had been asked to relax into a fundamental truth: love is real—and you can trust it. *Life repeats its lessons until you embrace a better path.*

The Eleventh Law of Karma: Patience

Love and Presence

Healing takes the time it needs

Have you ever sat back and wondered, *Why do bad things happen?*
Why is life not just one big happy
walk in the park—or a frisky run on
the beach?

I don't usually ponder questions
about bad things. Why would I? Life
almost always seems perfect to me.
There are good things to eat and to smell,
and lots of attention from Nicki almost anytime
I want it. (And I have ways of making her pay
attention!) There are walks with her and Doug,
and baths after, with thick, warm, fluffy towels.
And of course, there are so many things to love
here on our beautiful island: the sunrises and
sunsets, the birds in the breezes, the clouds and
the trees.

And then there's playing with my friends—

And that, right there . . . that's why I'm thinking today about why bad things have to happen.
It seems so unfair! Something very upsetting is

happening right now to my friend Jake. Nobody has told me this yet, but I know that Jake is dying. I know it because he's my best friend and I can feel him, even when he's at his house and I can't see him with my eyes. I do see him anyway—in a picture in my mind. His back paws are on the ground in this world. But his front paws are up on a low wall or a ledge or . . . something . . . that I'm pretty sure leads into the next world.

Where that next world is and what's in it, I'm not sure. I can't quite see it over that wall. Maybe it's a bigger, better playground where Jake will feel like himself again, cool and elegant in his stride, coat shining in the sun. Everyone looking on, admiring his style, like we all used to do any time Jake was around.

Ah, Jake. What a gentleman. What a friend to look up to—in more ways than one, for me. He's three times my height, of course, so I have to look up if I want to see into his eyes. But more than that, he's a big . . . a big . . . he's a big *life*. Big heart, big understanding, big vision to share. And he's been so generous in sharing it all with me.

Jake's life has been good, although it didn't start out that way. When he was little, he lived with someone who didn't even deserve to be around him, much less take care of him. Someone who kept him tied up to a doorknob in a garage *all* the time. It makes me furious every time I think about it! But then his real person, his favorite person, Kelly, came along, answering an ad in the newspaper. She hadn't intended to take him with her that day; she just went to see if she might like him. But she took one look at him tied up there and decided there was no way she was leaving without him. She loved him from the first minute. He does that to most people—and dogs. He just captures your heart from the get-go.

When Jake moves forward from here—when his back paws follow his front ones over the little wall—something bad will happen to me too. I'll miss him so much. I'm so sad now, I'm not even sure what sadder than this feels like, and I'm a little scared to find out.

I know this sounds strange, but I think when he goes to the next world, I might also feel relieved. Jake has been having such a hard time, for so long now, hurting a lot and not able to do the things he loves to do. He can't even come over to visit me anymore, even to just lie down in the grass together, and I know he wants to.

So my usually perfect life is not so perfect

right now. And it's hard just being myself today. It feels like my own skin doesn't fit me anymore. I tried sitting in my favorite chair. I turned in circles and dug into the cushion to make it just right, but I couldn't get comfortable. I went to my toy box and picked up all my favorites, one by one. I didn't care about any of them; they just wound up in a pile on the floor. I paced around the house, around and around and around and around, which left me panting. But then I stopped that too, because it seemed to worry Nicki. She picked me up and hugged me and gave me that "What's wrong?" look. So now I'm just sitting here quietly beside her.

Nicki knows I don't feel right, and I know she doesn't feel right. She's been giving me all of her time, and she even brought me my magic kitten. Mostly, I think Nicki has been busy trying to make me feel better, but I can see so clearly that she's as sad as I am. She loves Jake almost as much as I do. This bad thing . . . it's hard for her too. And all either of us can do is wait.

Jake used to tell me that friendship makes waiting easier. I think he was mostly talking about times when it's raining so hard you have to wait to go outside, or when it seems like it's taking your people forever to come home from their dinner out, maybe with a treat—things like that. It's easier, he told me, if there are at least two of you passing the time, listening to the clock tick, or watching the raindrops fall, taking little breaks to go to the water bowl and then coming back to your favorite spot to lie down.

So I'm sticking by Nicki, and she's sticking by me outside in my yard. It's nice out here to-day—it usually is, but today seems especially pretty. We can see big, puffy clouds moving slowly through the sky, and the blue is dotted with seagulls flying high. I'm pretty sure we can both smell fragrant flowers on the wind, and with my sharper nose, I can also smell damp dirt and earthworms, which I love. If something bad has to happen to Jake—and to me and to Nicki because of it—at least we have a peaceful place to be for now. A place where we can sit close together, and sigh when we need to, and wait for Jake to go on his way.

But wait . . . something is different now—something is changing. I can't find that picture of Jake in my mind anymore. I can't see him at all. There's just an empty space where he used to be. But I can *feel* him right here, so close to us.

Now Nicki is picking me up—I guess I've been barking, and . . . whining, I think. We have to say goodbye to Jake now. Jake's here, but he can't stay. He has to go.

Until we meet again, my dear friend. I love you.

My Shadow

It was November 2004. Doug and I had been married for nine years and had never spent a night apart. We had covered a lot of ground in those very full years. There were the kinds of ups and downs we all navigate in life. Much joy, some sorrow. Frustrations, yes, large and small. Lots of fun—trips to Las Vegas, rides on the water, and sunsets on the beach. Talking with each other about our plans, about life.

Always, it seemed, we were very busy as we built our business and our life together. We took pride in upgrading the house. Ours was one of the first homes in our neighborhood—built by Fred himself—across from the golf course, and we both loved the privacy of the location. This year, Fred's old house had a brand new roof and new impact windows and doors that we knew would be strong enough to stand up to a bad storm, even a hurricane, which was always something you needed to think about when you lived in the tropics.

I had more blessings than I could count, but right now . . . I was upset, and off balance. These days, I woke each morning with a cold, anxious feeling in the pit of my stomach.

It was Cheena; she had been sick for a while.

Cheena, my constant companion, the one who had shown me such devotion from the minute I brought her home. She had woven a thread of love through my life for so many years—seeing me through the sad, painful end of my bad marriage. There by my side as I came out of that dark time and found myself again, remembered who I really was. Along for the ride as I journeyed back to independence and strength. Right there with me to share my happiness as Doug entered my life—entered our lives, I should say—and then stayed.

Then she started having seizures. They were mild and far apart at first, but recently they had been getting much worse and more frequent, multiple times a day. They always followed the same pattern: First, she would get restless, nervous, shaky, and have trouble keeping her balance. Then, suddenly, she would fall on her side, muscles twitching throughout her body and otherwise unable to move, to stand. Perhaps the worst part was her high-pitched screams—that's the word for it; they weren't whines or yips. These spells only lasted for a minute, but when she was in one, there was nothing I could do for her. I couldn't ease her pain or fear in any way. It was so much for her body to go through, and I felt so helpless. All I could do was stroke her and talk to her and tell her it would be okay, and I didn't know if she could hear or feel me with her, if she even knew I was there.

I had delayed the inevitable decision for as long as I could, part of me hoping that the trend would somehow reverse itself, and she would get better, another part somehow knowing that her loss would be worse than I could possibly imagine and wanting to keep her with me as long as I could. But now, it was clear to me that time had run out. I couldn't stand her suffering any longer.

I had already called the vet to come to the house once, only to cancel. Cheena seemed to be getting better, I'd told myself that day . . . but really, I just lost my nerve. Now, today, the vet was on his way, for real.

Cheena lay on her bed looking up at me. She

was weak, exhausted, but she seemed calm, quiet, just resting. Of the two of us, I was far more distressed.

"I love you more than words can say, my Cheena Ling," I told her. "You were the first real love of my life." Tears rolled down my face faster than I could wipe them away. Long ago, I had realized that this little miracle of a dog had taught me what I needed to know about love in order to finally bring my own love into the world. To open my heart and share it, freely and generously. All I'd had to do was to follow her example. She had made it that easy.

Doug stood quietly by, available to help, but giving me the room I needed to let the feelings flow. He had known for some time now how bad her condition was, but he also knew I had to find my own way.

There was a knock at the door.

I gathered Cheena into my arms and held her tight as Dr. J. came in.

"It's time," he said as he looked at my tear-stained face. I could feel his compassion. I was glad I had chosen him years ago, and that I had asked him to do this at home instead of in his office. He went calmly about the business of preparing to give my shadow the relief she so badly needed, to help let her weary little body go.

I held Cheena in my lap until she took her final breath. Then Doug took her from me, wrapped a blanket around her, and walked outside to where the vet was now waiting.

I was wholly unprepared for the depth of loss I immediately felt. The house was so silent, so still. There was so much pain in my heart—it felt like it was being squeezed in a vise, or strangled. I felt a hollowness at the core of my being that I had never experienced before, a cold, dark, painful void.

It was hard to fathom what had just happened. Thirteen years of constant companionship, and then . . . nothing. It was so final. Irreversible. I couldn't fix it. There was no one I could call, nothing I could do. As I lay on the bed and sobbed my heart out, I kept thinking, I'm broken. I'm so broken now. How will I ever be whole again?

The Healing Balm of Time

When I look back on that day with the benefit of time—over more than a decade now—I know that wholeness does return. It's not that we forget the pain, or even that we stop feeling it. Anyone who has lost someone they love knows that grief has rhythms of its own, and it often comes in waves. But over time, those waves become easier to live with, part of the natural flow of a life lived with love. And I know that the depth of our loss is what ultimately allows us to understand, and reexperience, the fullness of the incredible gift of love we were granted. Knowing this makes it easier to float on the waves that come, lifted and supported by a full and grateful heart.

The evening Cheena died, as the sky grew dark, Doug turned on the dock lights, and I immediately thought, *That's good, in case she needs to find us in the dark.* I lit a candle for her too—this despite the fact that the sky was completely filled with stars.

When I think about that day now, the memory of all that light is what stays with me most. When she died, the energy of Cheena, the light of my life, merged into a brilliant symphony of light, blazing out of our world to join the stars.

With the gift of time, I can see that now.

The Twelfth Law of Karma: Inspiration

Hearts Opening

Love lifts us higher

Life always seems to have sur-
prises in store, doesn't it? No matter
how much the days might seem like
they're all the same. You're walking on
the same sidewalk and eating from the
same bowl as you did yesterday. You're
getting a shampoo after you've rolled in
the dirt—which you know will happen
every time you do that, but then something changes, something unexpected happens,
and you realize that no day is really the same as
the one before it.

Remember the tenth law of karma: change?
Well, I'm thinking about that again today, but for
a new reason.

In the weeks after Jake left us, I thought my
heart would always have a heavy, sorrowful
feeling. I couldn't imagine thinking about my
best friend and not feeling like the world he'd left
behind had gotten duller, sadder. But recently,
on one of those perfectly ordinary, same-same

kind of days—or really, on an ordinary night—
that dark heaviness I felt so sure would last forever, well . . . it felt different.

Nicki and I were in the backyard, looking up
at the stars on a moonless night. She had come
wide awake in bed just after midnight. In a split
second, she went from sound-asleep Nicki to
run-around-and-do-things Nicki. I heard her
stir suddenly, and then, in the dim light coming
through the window, I saw her eyelashes move
as she stared at the ceiling.

I should have known right then that a surprise
was coming. This wasn't normal; she's usually a
very good sleeper. She breathed in a big sigh
and swung her feet onto the floor and stood. I
stood up myself and went into fast-wag mode,
encouraging her to take me outside, which suddenly felt like the exact thing I wanted to do.
She smiled at me, and I knew she'd picked up on
what I wanted—she's smart that way.

Outside in the night, Nicki lay down on one
of those long chairs with the thick cushions,
wrapped in her light robe, and looked up at the
sky while I ran around sniffing. I made sure not
to go too far; she gets nervous if I roam more
than a few steps away. But the smells were ir-
resistible, so . . . vivid. It seemed like the air itself

was alive, and the grass had so many interesting stories to tell.

"It's beautiful tonight, isn't it, Karma? When there's no moon, there are so many stars."

I followed her gaze upward. I had to agree. It was very shiny up there.

"I've been thinking about my dad tonight, about his faith in me. He trusted that I could do anything I set my mind to. What a gift to me that was, Karma.

"He might as well have said, 'Look up into the stars, Nic, and pick whichever one you want. Pick a few of them, the ones you like best. Each one will set you on a new path of your own choosing, anytime you decide to make a change. They'll be your very own stars, there to guide only you, there to light each new step of your life.'"

Nicki's eyes were wet, but I knew she wasn't sad. She was feeling grateful for her dad—I was sure of that. Maybe she was even feeling grateful for all the winding paths she had taken to get here, to this place, to a backyard under a starlit sky, on an island she thought of as paradise and that felt like home.

Nicki had more to say. "I think one of those stars led me to you, Karma. And one led me to

Doug. Those were my best stars, hands down. Another one took me into a bad marriage, I guess so I would grow from lessons I could only learn the hard way. But then another one led me out of it, and I discovered just how strong I really was."

Nicki's voice was steady and soothing, and I was starting to get a little sleepy. I decided to close my eyes . . . just for a minute.

And that was when something very different happened.

A voice floated in on the breeze and reached my ears. *Jake is here, Karma, riding on the wind.*

Then a curious, damp sort of scent reached my nose, and I heard the words: *Jake is here, too, lying on the grass.*

I didn't know whose voice it was talking to my ears and my nose, but I knew the words it said were true. I knew it like I know every inch of my magic kitten. I knew it like I know the sound of Nicki's voice after I've done something that makes her laugh. Nicki sometimes talks about an inner knowing, a voice she says we all have if we will only listen for it. Maybe it was as simple as that.

All I really know is that it was true. Jake was here.

I looked up toward the distant palm trees silhouetted against the sky, watching as the fronds bent and danced. *Jake is up here in the leaves, Karma,* I very clearly heard.

It was then, the third time the voice spoke to me, that the heavy weight I'd thought would be a part of me forever lifted up out of my body. I felt it so clearly! It rose up, like a . . . like a great bird reaching for the highest treetops, up, up out of my heart, and away. Like a big, feathered creature rising and soaring away, maybe to a new nest, or maybe to another time and place.

I felt so different then, so light and . . . free! I hopped down from the chair and trotted into the grass again, sniffing the air and thinking about what had just happened.

Of course Jake is here, I realized as it all sank in. Jake has been right here beside me all along, no less an inspiration to me now than he was in the days when he walked by my side. Jake, my old teacher, my old friend, hasn't gone anywhere I can't find him. Our hearts melted together when I was only a pup, and our love connects us still.

Now I will lean on my friend's spirit to help me with my latest job—there's a new pup in town! Jake's human brought home an adorable cross between a golden retriever and a poodle, with bright, happy eyes and one of those faces that looks like it's always smiling. They named him Tanner. He's more soft, curly hair than anything else; when you wrestle with him you can feel how small his body is under all that fur.

Whenever Tanner's favorite human brings him out to play with me and my friends and all of their people, everybody wants to pick him up and squeeze him. Especially the women—they just can't seem to keep their hands off him. But he squirms and wriggles until they put him down because all he wants to do is run. And when he runs, he has only one destination in mind: me! Wherever I am, he wants to be there—I draw him like a magnet. So I've taken Tanner under my wing, and I feel a new sense of purpose now. When he comes over, I spend all my time showing him my favorite places in the yard, the ones with the best smells, and my favorite treats. It helps him calm down enough to be petted (at least for a minute).

One day when Tanner was over here it suddenly came to me: I'm teaching him how to be the best dog he can be, just as Jake taught me how to be the perfect companion. Tanner isn't here to replace Jake; he's here to lift us all up—and he's doing a grand job of it.

Sharing Stories

Not long after I lost Cheena, I decided to write a book. I didn't tell anyone I planned to do it. It just felt right to keep it to myself. It was almost as though if I talked about it, I would lose some of the energy behind the idea—and there was a lot of energy behind it. I got excited just thinking about it, and I wanted to hold that thrill of inspiration inside, keep it in a safe place, and help it grow even stronger.

I felt sure that I was meant to write this book. I've learned so many meaningful lessons on my journey through life, results of the experiences I've had along the pathways I traveled. I've faced and overcome disappointment and pain. I've grappled with fear and found courage. I've learned more about love than I ever imagined there was to know, and I continue to learn more each day. None of us lives inside the same skin, but we all possess a human heart in need of love, a human spirit in need of inspiration, a human mind in need of challenge and testing. We all get hurt, we all fall down, and we all experience feelings of triumph and joy when we stand up straight and strong again. We all have something to teach one another.

A Stranger Learns My Secret

One day Jean called me to extend an invitation.

"Hey, Nic," she said, "a friend of mine is hosting a get-together. It might be fun, or . . . it might just be strange, but either way, it'll be different."

"What in the world are you talking about, Jean?" I asked.

"It's my new friend Becky—you know, the one who took over the salon where I've been getting my hair cut for years. She's, well, I really like her a lot, but she's a little . . . out there sometimes. She's invited this psychic to do readings in the back room of the salon after it closes next Friday."

"A psychic . . . really?"

"Yeah, I know. But she invited me to attend and said I can bring a friend. Do you want to come with me? Supposedly, she talks to people who have passed away . . . people on the other side. And Becky says she's really good, that she always comes up with information that people swear she couldn't have gotten any other way."

"Well . . . I admit I have seen a couple of psychics before, and at least once they had some pretty interesting things to say. Do you think she's any good?"

"She might be—my friend thinks so at least. She could be the real deal, and think how hard you'd kick yourself if you learned she really could talk to people on the other side and you hadn't gone to see her for yourself. Plus, even if she is a fake, it would be a lark. Good fun. C'mon, let's go."

When she put it that way, it did sound like it could be exciting, and I agreed to go. But I made up my mind in advance that if this woman wound up doing any kind of reading for me, I wouldn't give her a thing to go on. I'd be one of her toughest customers.

We arrived to find a room that had been well prepared for an intimate gathering, with soft lighting and cushy chairs. I dragged Jean to the very back of the rows of chairs.

"Don't give her any clues, Jean, if she calls on you," I whispered.

Jean laughed and put her finger to her lips, shushing me.

When we were all settled, about fifteen of us in all, a pleasant looking, older woman with short hair walked to the front of the room. She was slender and casually dressed in a simple blouse and jeans—she didn't exactly look like Madame Zorba to me. She introduced herself as Antonia and said she had been given the gift of a certain kind of clairvoyance. "I am in touch with people who want to communicate from the other side, and I can hear them and see images of things they're thinking of," she said. "Other clairvoyants work only on this side of the veil. They might be able to tell you where you lost your favorite earrings. If that's why you came here tonight, I'm sorry, but I can't help you with that."

She smiled as a ripple of laughter moved through the room. I found myself smiling too.

"I'm going to open myself to messages now. When I get something, I'll ask if it speaks to anyone in the room."

The first message that came through was puzzling. Antonia was hearing from someone about a shiny blue dog with black eyes. Oddly specific, I thought. A woman in the audience gasped, and Antonia turned to face her.

"Does that make some kind of sense to you?"

"Yes," said a young woman with long, dark hair. "It does. My niece had a toy just like that, a dog. Handmade by her mom, covered with royal blue satin, of all the things to give a child. Black, shiny buttons for the eyes. She . . ." Her voice broke. "My niece died two years ago, just twelve years old. We were all devastated."

"Ah, I see. Of course you were. That's so very, very sad. But now your niece wants to tell you something. She says it's important."

The dark-haired woman waited.

"She says you've been thinking about going to . . . I'm not sure. Another city? Another country? But you don't think you should leave your brother, her father. She says he's doing much better now, that it's been long enough since she passed over. He's made a little peace with it, and he'll be okay if you go. She says you can leave now if you still want to."

The young woman clasped her hands to her mouth. She nodded silently. Then she returned her hands to her lap.

"Okay," she said. "Tell Poppy that I heard her, and thank her for me . . . and I love her."

If a group of fifteen women, mostly strangers, can share goosebumps and tears, well, we were busy sharing. Jean and I turned to each other with open mouths.

The next two messages were easier for all of us to hear. A woman's mother, long passed after living a full life into her nineties, told her daughter that she had worked in a cubicle in an office for long enough. That she didn't have to be so scared of quitting her job to pursue her dream of becoming an artist, that she would receive enough support to follow that dream. Another woman's ex-husband came through to apologize for what he had put her through during their brief, argumentative marriage. These messages seemed more ordinary to me. Lots of people have office jobs and would rather be artists; lots have had short, bad marriages and would love to hear their ex-spouse apologize. I could feel my skepticism start to return.

Then Antonia spoke again. "Now I'm seeing . . . well, I don't really understand it. . . . I'll just describe it. I'm seeing a jar of pickles falling off a kitchen shelf and smashing to the floor," she said. "It's a big mess. There are . . . eleven pickles on the floor."

I froze in my seat. She was speaking to me.

Return to Bromley

In February 2012, my father died. He had been sick with Alzheimer's and deteriorating for many years. No one was surprised when he finally passed. Still, it was hard to receive the phone call; I would never see his smile again.

Doug and I packed our bags and flew to London, and then drove to Bromley for the funeral, held in the Good Shepherd Church. As people entered the church, Mum recounted that she and Dad had gone to the Good Shepherd Primary School right next door, and that years later they fell in love over table tennis at the Good Shepherd Youth Club. They had married in the very church where we were standing, in a ceremony that—unlikely, even impossible, as it seems—was even presided over by the very same man now officiating the funeral, Father Butler.

The service began, and my dad's coffin was carried in. At that exact moment, the children in the school next door were let out for recess and ran to the playground, the same playground my dad used to play on when he was a child. You could hear them shouting and laughing as Father Butler read scripture. I couldn't help but imagine my dad smiling.

Life seemed to have come full circle in this town where everyone knew everyone else. As the ceremony wrapped up, I was filled with a deep pride and felt blessed to be part of such history and kinship. I had moved away from my hometown to create a new life for myself, but that didn't mean I wouldn't be forever bound to my roots.

We heard from people who had loved Dad, and then it was my turn to remember the man who had shaped my world:

Toward the end, Dad didn't remember very much, but he remembered four things well. The story of his brother, the great boxer; he never forgot the story, only that he had already told it to you. Then there were the names, and he remembered three. There was Maureen, the wife of my mum's brother. She had sat by his bedside and read to him from the history books about Bromley. After a while, everyone became Maureen—she must have made a big impact with those stories. Then there was Pickle, the nickname of his youngest granddaughter. He said her name often, as the thought of her made him smile and laugh. Finally, while he had forgotten so much, he never forgot the name of my beloved first dog, Cheena. She too made a lasting impact on his journey.

It is the heart that makes the man, and my dad has always shown me kindness, generosity, and love. He brought me up to believe in myself and to believe I could do anything if I really wanted to. It has taken me far, to new experiences, a new country, a new life. That strength to take on new beginnings was a gift.

May you live on through those who love you, Dad, and know that I will always remember you singing that quirky song, "When I Need You" by Leo Sayer—*When I need you, I just close my eyes and I'm with you* . . .

. . .

We got back to Marco Island early enough for Doug to check in at work and grab some groceries while I took time to unpack and regroup. I still had a lot to process. A friend had told me before we left for the funeral that I'd never be the same after losing my dad. I remembered questioning her. "Why would it affect who I am? I like my world and myself right now. Why would I change?" But it turned out that she was right. In a way I couldn't yet put my finger on, I would be different now.

I sat at the kitchen table with a cup of hot tea

and Karma by my side. I reached down to stroke the soft white fur around her ear, noticing how loud the ticking of the wall clock sounded. As I reached down to lift Karma onto my lap, I noticed I was sitting on something. It was some crumpled papers: a photo of my dad wrapped in the eulogy I had written for his service. I carefully smoothed the edges of his picture. After taking a sip of my tea, I decided to read the words of the eulogy out loud to Karma while she listened—I can always count on Karma to listen. When I read the part about granddaughter Pickle, Karma pricked up her ears as though something had startled her. Before I could get another word out, there was a heart-stopping CRASH! Karma and I both jumped.

I spun around to my left, where a row of shelves lined the pantry wall. A jar of pickles had fallen to the floor and smashed. And now eleven pickles lay splattered on the floor.

I was positive I had stored that jar a good distance away from the edge of that shelf. I could feel my dad's presence and I wondered how much energy it had taken him to make that jar move. Clearly, he wanted my attention.

Instead of cleaning up the mess, I closed my eyes and simply let myself hear him.

"Turn on the music, Nic," I heard him say from

deep inside me. "Whenever you need me, just listen for me. I'll always be there."

Dad's Advice

I had managed to start breathing again as I sat there in the back row at the psychic reading.

"That message is for me," I blurted out. Jean's head whipped around, and she looked at me, wide-eyed. She was the only other person in the room who knew why.

"It's coming from a man, an older man, who I think was very close to you," Antonia said. "Does that seem right?"

"Yes," I said.

"Does a broken jar of pickles mean something to you?"

"Yes."

"And what is that meaning?"

"I . . . it doesn't matter. I know who sent you that picture. It's my dad. Does he have a message for me?"

Antonia was quiet, her head tilted to one side as if listening for something here in this world.

"He says, 'Keep writing in longhand.' Does that make sense?"

"Yes, it does," I said. "Is there anything else?"

"He's saying that people are going to tell you to write it on the computer, but you shouldn't listen to them. You need to feel the shapes of the letters and words with your hand and arm as you write. And he says he's proud of you, and that what you're writing will be both a comfort and an inspiration to others.

"Are you writing a book?" Antonia asked.

"Yes!" I admitted, at last releasing my secret to the world.

The time had come, like it or not, to share my news with a close friend—and a group of complete strangers. A feeling of joy welled up inside of me, lifting me higher and stronger. My dad knew I was writing a book, and he was as supportive of me as ever. Now my good friend knew. Even people I had never met knew my secret. Maybe someday, without even knowing the book was mine, one of them would read it.

It was time to start writing in earnest now, right out in front of everybody, right out loud, with my favorite pen in my hand, and Good Karma by my side.

Dear new friend,

I hope you have found me to be
a good companion as you traveled
through the twelve laws of karma
with Nicki and me. We have been
so happy to share this story with
you—and are glad you gave yourself
the gift of time so you could sit down
and read it. In this book, we wanted to
show you that all the roads we travel are
meaningful ones, each in its own way.
That even when things get difficult, we
can learn from our troubles and grow
stronger because of them. As we absorb
these twelve lessons of the universe, we
grow in many ways. We become more fully

who we are meant to be in this world. And if we learn these lessons well, at the same time we are growing into ourselves—becoming more confident, more awake and alive—we also get better at opening our hearts. We learn how to embrace all that life has to offer: the pets and people who enter our world and the many other joys that this mysterious and wonderful universe sends our way. And from the loved ones who leave before us, we can even learn how to be kind to ourselves when life feels heavy which, when we are left alone, can sometimes be the most challenging lesson of all.

I am grateful that you were here with us for a while. Now it's time for you to continue the journey on your own, and so I send you off with all of my best wishes. But before I let you go, I want to pass along something important I've learned, something I feel from time to time, usually when I'm sitting quietly in my favorite front-porch chair, or out on that really long chair in the backyard, at night under a starry sky.

If we know love is the only thing we are taking with us, then love we must be, to attract love and light. It is our destiny.

Love,
Good Karma

Acknowledgments

Help always comes through to us if we accept it, if we listen. The Universe brought me a team of champions to help me write my story, a powerful force for someone who was about to take a leap not meant for one! I am so grateful to have met everyone who was part of this journey.

Sheridan McCarthy, my writer, editor, and friend, who has softly held my life in her hands for two and half years and watched me turn my book inside out and upside down. You came along and wonders happened as you witnessed this birth and cleaned up this baby more than once! Your light has brightened every page.

My mystical friend Mist. The universal laws have taken us both on an incredible journey. Your talents place you among the stars, and you help make others shine.

Kelly Notaras, a great author and someone I'm honored to say is an editor and coach of mine. That day I met you with Wayne Dyer, everyone swarmed around you like bees. I reached in, grabbed a business card, and then left. You just never know when someone you've never met before will change your life forever. It can happen on any given day; be ready! Love, Good Karma wouldn't be the same without you.

Jill Yris, it was my story that reached you to the core and hit a note, but it was your magic eye and sense of humor that made me feel like dancing. And how sweet that Jolie's love of a belly rub found its way into the book.

Amy Hayes, you tied the knot and shared the love all over the cover. I will celebrate your kindness and warm spirit every year. It is not often you meet someone special who shares your day— "Leo" sister!

Pat Verducci, my writing coach, the first one to listen to my story. You taught me about the hero's journey and helped me discover mine.

Elisabeth Rinaldi, thank you for the paw prints that brought an extra shine to Love, Good Karma.

Barbara Webster because I know you read every word with care. I finally trust in my English teacher enough to keep both feet on the ground!

To my sweet Karma, who reminds me to look up at the stars and enjoy the wonder of it all.

And to my husband. The beginning, the middle, and the end all happened because I am so loved.

Made in the USA
Columbia, SC
20 April 2021